NETHERWORLD WAYS

By

Terry H.S. Wallace

NETHERWORLD WAYS

by

Terry H.S. Wallace

Rabbit Publications
Camp Hill, Pennsylvania 17011-2947
2013

Published in the United States of America by Rabbit Publications

ISBN: 978-0-9701375-6-2

Cover and book design by Accurance

Dedication:

For those who want to know what's really going on, for our struggle is not against flesh and blood, but against the rulers, against the authorities, against the powers of this dark world and against the spiritual forces of evil.

Acknowledgements:

The author is greatly indebted to several writers and friends who contributed to the preparation of *Netherworld Ways*, through their various suggestions and insightful critiques: Phil Reemes, Leslie Thompson, Gail Varney, and Marjorie Woodward.

"But mark this: There will be terrible times in the last days. People will be lovers of themselves, lovers of money, boastful, proud, abusive, disobedient to their parents, ungrateful, unholy, without love, unforgiving, slanderous, without self-control, brutal, not lovers of the good, treacherous, rash, conceited, lovers of pleasure rather than lovers of God – having a form of godliness but denying its power."
-2 Timothy 3:1-5

TABLE OF CONTENTS

FROM FAST TIME IN NO TIME

*My Friends, time goes apace. We are wearing off and in a little while
we shall be here no more. Time will be gone and the day of your visitation quickly over.*
-William Penn

The truth is: one day you wake up dead.

I did.

I can hear you thinking: "Now how did you know you were dead?"
Right?

Let me count the ways. Check my pulse: you'll find that regular code
is gone. My blood pressure zero over zero. Not the faintest ghost of a
breath on the mirror held under my nose. My face flaccid, expressionless,
that telltale absence of personality. The odor of feces and urine soaking
my briefs, the body having voided its contents. Consider my eyes, the
cloudiness of congealing aqueous humor.

OK, OK, I'll stop – you've heard enough – but before I do I'll detail
just one more: that small creature like a poison toad, wrapped in rags. He
squats at the head of my prone body, inspects it, probes with a filthy
forefinger here and there, then rocks back on his heels, satisfied.

"Yep!" He rips. "Definitely, indubitably, done-in dead."

~~~~~

I opened one eye, brow cocked, and considered the pocked and
scarred face starring down at me. "Well, what'd you expect?" My
question barely a whisper.

"Exactly that! No more; no less." His rummy, red-rimmed eyes
continued to consider me. "You were a handsome one once. Clean you
up a little – wash off the dried blood around the ears and nose, change
your diapers – and we'll see what we have here." He unfolded from his
squatting position and I realized he was a short little fellow, perhaps five-
foot-two, stubby and rude looking like Napoleon – that's Napoleon on
Elba, mind you, reduced and eaten out by syphilis. I was fully awake now

1

– dead, mind you, but fully awake. Remember what I said: "One day you wake up dead." Well, at least I'd awakened! Dead.

Then he stooped, face inches from mine, lifting my shoulders. "Let's get you back on your feet, such as they are." He heaved and, miracle of miracles, I was up standing.

"No miracle about it," he spat in the dust at my feet, "and you're not upstanding," he chortled. "Come along now!"

"Wait!"

"No one waits on anyone here," He turned his back and padded away. "Now come along!"

I came, but wobbling forward on my newly dead feet, I whined, "Slow down. I didn't even catch your name."

"As if it matters here," he tossed the words back over his shoulder. "And weren't you always the one living on Fast Time?"

I steadied myself with a hand on what felt like the slick sweating surface of a wall, and murmured, "as if it matters now."

"It doesn't once it gets you here," came the retort.

"Names! Names matter!" I shouted at his back. "What's your name?"

"*Au contraire:* names mean absolutely nothing here." He stopped, turned, considered me for a long moment, then seemed to relent. "Faust." His exhalation was barely audible.

"Fast? What kind of name is that?"

He locked me with his eyes and uttered with more care and definiteness: "Faust, you fool."

"Faustus?! The great genius, intellect extraordinaire, bold mind and bolder spirit. You can't – he was tall, handsome, a dash of salt, and heavy with pepper. The very measure of man's greatness, an independent superego born to rule…". I knew I babbled, but Faustus! Here before me? This shriveled up prune of a man, humpback, and more than a little degenerate?

"No," came his firm reply. "Just *Faust*."

"I knew a Dr. Faustus."

"NO you didn't," he shot back with such energy and anger, I decided to bail out of the topic.

"Whatever. What's a name anyway," I murmured

"Nothing," he growled and turned to march on through the dull gray fog that surrounded us.

"Where are we going?" I almost whimpered it, looking around, seeing nothing but drifting phantasms of mist against the otherwise unrelieved grayness.

"My place."

"Your place? You've a place? What kind of place would that be?"

"You'll see."

"You're telling me to be patient, right?"

"Wrong. You can be as impatient as you want. It makes no difference." Faust stopped to light the stub of a ragged stogy, drew a long puff, coughed, and threw it aside. I watched the glowing tip arc and fall, until in winked out. Faust bent double, holding his knees, the cough now a downright vicious hack. He spat something dark, spat again something even larger, and finally drew himself partially erect again.

"OK. On to your place, wherever and whatever that is."

~~~~~

We traveled through the cloying grayness over rough ground, our direction always headed downward. Every few steps I'd stumble and mumble that I hadn't my hiking legs yet. Faust would just grunt and continue on ahead. Problem was: I couldn't keep up his pace – a pace that was surprisingly brisk and impatient for a creature in his degraded condition. Winded and weary – perhaps from a life of too much booze, tobacco, coke, and meth? - I finally sank to my knees. Faust marched ahead to the very edge of my vision, then halted, turned, and growled, "Come on, wimp."

"No," I groaned.

"Typical. First the booze and tobacco, then the coke and meth – we get too many of you stone heads here!" Faust trotted back, leaned over me, examined me with his red-rimmed eyes, and murmured to himself, "Cowards just ain't got no gumption."

That stung and I gathered enough strength to thrust him away. "Go away and leave me be! I don't need you, never wanted you. I've never needed anyone: Get scarce!" I literally spat in his face.

He recoiled, gave me a murderous glare, turned his back grousing to himself, "Chief's right as usual: no deed goes unpunished." In seconds, Faust had disappeared, swallowed by the gloom.

3

My first reaction was "good riddance!" After what seemed like – no, I won't say an eternity though I am on occasion given to both clichés and hyperbole – I realized my first was not my best reaction. My "good riddance" was as good as it first felt, but then I surveyed my surroundings, if you could call them such: nothing but drifting shades of dark in every direction. The ground felt chill, the air chill, I myself obviously chill and growing more so as I contemplated my plight. Without a thought, I'd sent my only guide, if I could call him that, packing, and now that I thought about it, I'd no idea what my next step should be. I took several tentative steps in several uncertain directions, but nothing changed in my nothing landscape, except the depth of my foreboding. I momentarily slumped to the soil again, only to jump up when something slithered by my hip.

That's when I panicked, whining, "Faust. Faust! Come back. I didn't mean it." I heard nothing but the suspiration that passes for silence here. "Faust, damn you! FAUST! I beg of you! Don't leave me...."

"What in hell do you want, you little turd?" I started and whirled around: Faust! It was Faust, still with his murderous demeanor, but at least I wasn't alone.

"Oh, thank...," He slapped his filthy palm across my mouth, smothering the next word into an incoherent grunt. "DON"T you DARE utter that here! Get anymore stupid and I'll leave you here and not come back."

"Please," I dropped to my knees, "please. Hear me out. I'm sorry."

"Sorry? Sorry, no apologies accepted here either."

"You were always my author, your bold style...."

"My banal self-promotion and self-adulation, you mean."

"No! I swear! You are, of all writers, the most honored and revered...."

"Oh, please," Now Faust was begging, "none of that means anything here."

"I can pay you well!"

"With what? You're bankrupt! Anyway, money has no meaning here either."

"P-L-E-A-S-E!" I screamed. "Hear me out."

"I'm hearing. I'm hearing. I'm almost deaf after that shriek! What in hell do you want?"

I caught my breath. "Be my Virgil, please."

"VIRGIL!?"

That seemed to have offended Faust more than any of my earlier words and he appeared ready to turn heel and disappear again, for good.

"I mean: my guide…," I whimpered.

"There ain't no guides here either. Never were. Never will be. No help at all. No one needs a guide here. No one's going any place. *Comprendre?*"

I didn't want to, but obviously had to. "Yes." My *yes* was all but inaudible.

Faust cocked his head, then nodded, and growled, "No guide, but you can choose to follow me or not. You used to follow anyone, especially the ones in skirts."

"Right," I mouthed almost inaudibly.

"And men with money."

"Hmm," I winced.

"It's up to you."

Meekly, "I'll follow."

"You're sure now?"

"Yes. Lead me on."

Faust turned away, "You always were a follower."

5

BLACK AND NIGHT AND GRAY

"It is easy to go down to hell; night and day the gates of Dark Death stand wide;
but to climb back up again, to retrace one's steps to the open air,
there lies the problem,
the difficult task".
-Virgil

I followed the undulating shadow of Faust's back as we descended. As the grayness that embraced us darkened toward something denser, more somber, he'd lit the stub of a torch which spit and smoked and hardly gave sufficient light for our way. Worse, he held it down in front of him, probably to see where he placed his steps. What dim uneven light it cast outlined his darker form with a lurid purple aura. I placed each of my own steps with care so as to avoid slipping, tripping, or falling again, a care that anesthetized my sense of time, so that after what seemed like hours, but may have been just minutes, I became aware of the vaguest contrast ahead, a contrast to the blackness we had entered and through which we made our way. I'll never be such a cliché monger to call it "the light at the tunnel's end" – merely less darkness that resolved slowly over time into what appeared to be a growing gray orifice. Faust murmured something to himself as he bumbled ahead, and I closed the distance between us to catch his mantra-like words:

> Black and night and gray:
> Gray is all we'll know today.
> Black and night and gray.

He uttered it with a grim monotony that oppressed me and I soon dropped behind simply to escape it.

What had first appeared as a dot of gray in the blackness ahead of us began to resolve itself into a larger and larger circle as we made our way toward it and, finally, as we neared the exit or entrance (I wasn't sure which), the tunnel's end resolved into a broad and towering....

Yes, I must use the word again: *orifice*. An immense maw punctuated here and there by stalactites and stalagmites that dwarfed us to insignificance. We stood, two miniscule figures on the lip of the opening and surveyed the landscape below us, an immense plain that stretched away in every direction until the vague gray horizon swallowed it. And on the plain itself? A city larger, grander, than I'd ever seen before – and yes, I'd seen New York and Moscow and Tokyo and Calcutta, Cairo and Chicago, Mexico City and Baghdad! Some aspects of the place – its restless din, its teeming millions, its explosive sprawl …its incredible clutter - bore a vague resemblance to Los Angeles, but the City of Los Angeles it was not. The scene immediately below us was a helter-skelter conglomeration of shacks and concrete block buildings, crowded densely together. Few were more than two or three stories, some clearly abandoned and leaning toward collapse, a few charred and blighted by fire, most drab gray and perhaps a century or two old. Beyond these stood a handsome gathering of towers, soaring mirrors into the haze over the metropolis. And over all rose the hum and thrum of heavy traffic and heavier industry. To my right, I could see, stretching to the very edge of my vision, the belching stacks of a host of mills, plants, and factories, boiling black smoke skyward. *Desultory order at best,* came to my mind, *product of rapid, yea, rampant growth that had consumed the plain. Consumed the plain* – problem was I had no idea whether it really "consumed the plain," for how far the plain stretched was nowhere evident and I could see no boundaries in the distance like mountains or a sea coast.

To the left, at the very edge of my vision, I saw the shadow of an immense complex, brooding, overbearing, on a steep rise over a great cluster of barrios, slums, and warrens. Something intrigued me about its design (yes, it did possess a very distinct design, unlike much of the general metropolis), something I vaguely recognized, but couldn't quite name. It impressed me both by its incredible grandeur, a grandeur seemingly quite out-of-place, even in the most imperial of capitals, yet unmistakably dominant, the obvious hub of the bold scatter before me. I felt its draw and hoped somehow we might be headed there.

"Come along," Faust ordered.

I didn't move, still rooted in amazement: "What *is* this place?"

"No place in particular. Any place you wish. How about we call it 'home'?"

"Oh, come on," I was annoyed at his evasions. "Get real."

"I'm always 'real'," he felt himself as if he was making sure he still was, then looked up and smirked. "Call it what you want, your 'forbidden city' perhaps? Or your big shouldered hog town? How about your 'naked city' – maybe just what I call it, 'my kinda town.'" Faust tripped a little jig and cut a caper at this latter.

"And others?"

"Others what?" Faust returned.

"What do others call it?"

"Lots of things!"

"Like?"

"Everything!"

"Oh, come on!" I was more than impatient and he delighted in being the tease.

"How about 'Belching Bertha?' Or 'The Grand Ol' Whore?' Maybe 'Big Babylonia!'"

I gave up, knowing I'd not get a straight answer out of him.

"You have to admit, it's quite a view," Faust croaked, extinguishing his torch in a stagnant pool. "The way down's over here." He motioned left and I saw a long winding road, at first rather precipitous, one with dozens of cut backs leading down to the plain below and the city's edge. "That road twists so much, it'd break a snake's back!" He chortled. I wasn't impressed or amused by his attempt at humor, but he ignored me, stepped forward, and we continued our descent.

Again, like the tunnel, the road down proved long and circuitous. We rested at various turn-outs along the way and I got a far better sense of the city than I had from the heights. *Vast* was no longer an operative description. *Gargantuan* was better. As we entered its streets, the place seemed a cross between Gotham City and Gomorrah, Shanghai and Sodom, Baghdad and Babylon all mixed together. It possessed Gotham's dark menace and Gomorrah's gross carnality, Shanghai's aimless multitudes and Sodom's grotesque sexuality, Baghdad's shambled mass and Babylon's gray and dusty slavery.

I had no way of knowing whether the district we entered was typical or not. I hoped untypical because it was so remarkably depressing. The buildings were constructed of an unrelieved gray concrete, defaced with obscene and profane artless graffiti. Many of the structures appeared unstable, with serious cracks and crumbling. Whole blocks of empty tenements leaned over us and the street itself was strewn with garbage and abandoned furniture, burned out appliances and filthy mattresses. The only object somewhat attractive was a small gold lettered street sign. I walked over to get a closer look and found it damaged, *Boulevard of the Ange-*. Whatever more there might have been was splintered off, and though I surveyed the area, the missing section had disappeared. *Well enough*, I thought in the next minute as I did a fancy two step to avoid stepping on a corpse lying face down in an open sewer, then another, and I turned to Faust for an explanation. He hadn't seemed to notice them.

Faust, instead, was considering the way ahead and apparently didn't like what he saw – though what he saw was unclear. "Time to go to ground," he whispered and stepped to a chipped and splintered door. He rapped the wood hard and gave it a swift kick: "Come on! Damn you!" Shuffles and scrapes from the inside told us something stirred: the door inched open and Faust slammed his shoulder against it throwing the old crone inside to the floor.

"Hey!" She shrieked, then saw who it was she addressed and her demeanor changed in an instant: "My lords, please. Come in. Wash your feet. Spend the night. Do *they* know you're in the neighborhood?" She eased herself painfully up, rubbing her bruised shoulder.

Stunned at Faust's rude violence, I nearly stepped forward to steady her, but he cut me off, "Of course, they know we're here! Nothing gets by them!"

"To the back rooms, then. I and my boys will handle the door." She pushed me toward the building's rear. Without so much as a *thank you*, Faust slammed through the intervening doors, until he reached a dim and stinking kitchen. He grabbed a chunk of cheese and a fistful of hardtack, while I stood, bewildered, in the corner.

"What...?"

Faust held up his hand as he masticated a mouthful and muffled: "Wait for it!"

"Wait...?" And then I knew: wait for the pounding, which boomed through the house and shook the rafters, such as they were. Wait for the splintering wood and breaking glass. Wait for the rough demand.

"Where are the men who just came here?! Bring them out so we can have sex with them!"

My ear against the kitchen door, I could hear the old crone trying to dissuade them. "They're guests, my friends, *Lords* from the palace!"

"*Lords*, my eye. That was old Faust came in here and it's about time he suffered a come down." Faust shouldered past me and disappeared up the hall. "Faust, you bastard…," a crack and slam told me something had happened. I went forward and found Faust and the old crone's boys were laying into the gang at the door. Their ringleader was out on the ground, his teeth scattered around him, and Faust cudgeled another of the gang with a skull splitting whack.

"There are good little girls next door," Faust hissed. "Take them and git." *They got.*[1]

~~~~~

As we left next morning, we found no sign of men, but several women whistled and beckoned to us seductively: "How about a little *lordly* sex," one purred, stark naked, hips gyrating. Faust stopped, considered the invitation for a few seconds, and then spat: "Sorry. No time, girls. On a mission for The Chief." Even as he grabbed my arm and trotted me out of range, their disdain shocked me: enough rotten eggs and vegetables for a fair sized breakfast and enough obscenities for a long and dreary pornographic novel.

"They don't like you very much," I quipped.

'They don't have to and you don't either," was Faust's tart response.

They were soon far behind us, but the squalidness of the district was not. Every block had at least one bar, but a monotony pervaded them all – half-lit neon signs, scuffed and pitted doors, discordant and irritating music. Once or twice I thought I heard jazz as I passed an open doorway, but jaded, unpleasant, the riffs uncertain and jumbled. As it punished my ears, all I could think was: "Don't play it again, Sam. Shoot the piano player…, and the saxman, and the drummer, and…."

"A bar on every block, sometimes two," Faust observed. "Could be worse!"

"Worse?"

"No bars at all," he grinned, exposing his yellow broken teeth. "They're not very creative in the naming department, though." I surveyed a half dozen signs, most of them faded and discolored: *The Bottle, The Jug,*

The Glass, The Pitcher, The Mug.… I had to agree. The "M" on the last sign had burned out, leaving only *The -ug.*

"Watch where you step!" Faust pointed to a noxious stream down the left side of the street. I did a quick two step and barely avoided getting the muck on my shoes. The stench was growing so bad in this area my stomach gave that uncertain heave that precedes a full release of its contents. "And watch the windows. Somebody is always emptying a chamber pot." As if on cue, I felt the light spray of droplets from a disgusting splash a few steps behind me – and heard a hoarse voice crow: "Missed ya!" Apology? Or regret? I couldn't tell from the tone, but suspected the latter.

I finally got up my gumption and asked, "Where we headed?"

Faust tossed the answer over his shoulder: "You, sir, have a special audience with The Chief! Quite an honor, if I do say so. What did you do to get it?"

"Do? I have no idea! I don't even know a chief."

"*The Chief.*" Faust corrected me with particular emphasis. Well, He knows *you* and He doesn't see just anybody. Most wait eons and many still are." Faust eyed me with a certain respect – or was it suspicion? We trudged on in silence for several exhausting, repulsive miles, then stopped to lift a couple of glasses in *The Cracked Jug.* Faust had turned into the doorway, declaring the place to be "better than most." Its beer proved warm and liquor watered down, but enough of the latter gave me backbone to continue my slow and quiet interrogation of my guide. When we left an hour later, I pondered Faust's claim further: If *The CJ*, as it was known locally, was "better than most," how bad could *bad* be. I decided I didn't want to find out.

"This Chief…," I began.

"*The* Chief. The one and only. The Lord and Master of this whole vast wide, wild, and wooly world." Faust emphasized that fact with an expansive sweep of his hand.

"*The Chief.*" I began again. "What's He like?" I could see Faust glance at me out of the corner of his eye, as if taking a surreptitious measure. Or was it that he wasn't quite sure how much he should say? I suddenly wondered if I wanted to know what was coming, feeling something like maggots writhing in my stomach. In the next second, I shook it all off, like a dog emerging from his swim. Why should I be nervous? Faust said

11

special and *quite an honor.* I need only be nervous about measuring up, making a good impression, and even that didn't seem too important if my reputation had preceded me. Yet, that thought gave me further pause: *What reputation?* I didn't have a reputation, at least not in a very positive sense, not in the sense that would make a leader interested in me.

I was so busy with my thoughts that I'd not noticed that Faust had chosen not to answer me, but now aware of it, I stopped and faced him, speaking rather plaintively: "The Chief. I need to know a little to be prepared properly to meet him." Was it my sincerity that moved Faust? Or my simple need? Or some twisted motivation of his own? Whatever it was, he decided to speak.

"The Chief. Well, now. What's He like? What should I say?"

And what shouldn't you say? I oddly found myself thinking. Again, I shook it off and tried to concentrate on his carefully chosen words: "Some say He's a rough and ready rag-tag rebel. Others: a rough hand at the helm, tough on His friends and cruel to His enemies. He knows hate burns a long time when its hard and betrayal is the coin of every realm." Faust stopped, as if searching for further words, so I interjected my own concern.

"What'll He *look* like? His demeanor. What should I expect?"

"You mean, will He be red in tooth and claw?" Faust smiled his broadest broken smile, a remarkably wicked grin if I do say so myself.

"Be serious!" I didn't like being played with.

"I *am* being serious." Then Faust seemed to reconsider and relent. "Look. The Chief's a fashion bug, a style setter. You never know what costume He'll choose to show up in. Sometimes He's a Generalissimo, sometimes a rather staid Chancellor, sometimes He likes the robes and appears like the pope for an audience. Don't expect anything as degraded as a Hell's Angel biker, though: quite below Him!" Amazing. *This was more like it*, I thought. At least I was getting some useful information. "He once appeared as a horse's ass," Faust chortled.

"You joke!"

"No. Not really. He did it for an audience with a horse's ass!"

"You're still pulling my leg," just a hint of irritation in my voice.

"Whatever. What I'm saying is that The Chief will choose the costume best suited to the audience. Don't be surprised – and don't be shocked unless He chooses to shock you."

Now it was my turn to retort: "Whatever." Faust was playing with me again and I could expect no more information, but that was OK. I'd gotten enough.

ON THE BOULEVARD OF THE ANGEL OF LIGHT

As I trudged on behind Faust through the dark, stinking, depressing streets of the barrio, I realized I still did not know where we were headed. Faust's answer to my question had been "To The Chief," but He was a person, not a place. Were we headed for some secret rendezvous? Another of Faust's dubious safe houses? Or a government office? Or? That answer meant more and more to me the deeper we penetrated this slum, for I was becoming dead tired of dragging my dead feet around sewers, side stepping debris fields, and watching that I didn't stumble into a pothole and break my ankle.

I planted my aching feet and grunted, "Answer me this."

"Answer you what?" Faust growled as he continued forward. You didn't ask anything."

"Where *are* we going?!"

"To The Chief, like I said, *comprendre?*"

"Chief's a person, not a place, *comprendre?*"

My snideness stopped Faust in his tracks and he turned his evil little blood shot eyes on me: "Well, well, well, got a smarty-pants here, don't we. Tired of our little stroll already?" He ambled back, until we were almost nose-to-nose, and studied me, but I wouldn't be put off.

"I'm dead tired of the muck and mire here."

"That's 'cause you're dead!" His breath nearly gagged me.

"Dead or not, I want to know where we're going – Timbuktu, the dark side of the moon, or where no man has gone before?"

Faust turned away with an "ain't you jolly!"

I didn't move and threatened, "I won't move until I know."

"Even if the skitter bugs infest ye and the locals feast on your body?" He was moving away at a good clip and I made to follow in a tardy, desultory fashion, unsure of whether he was joking or not.

"Be fair! It's a legitimate question!" I shouted.

"I'm never fair and nothing's legitimate here, *comprehende?*"

"*Is it too much to ask?*" I was exasperated in the extreme.

Faust turned, seemed to be searching his mind as he quizzically massaged his chin. "Hmmm. Guess not. Faust pointed at something ahead, but very well out of our field of vision: "There."

"Oh, for...! Where's there?"

He pointed emphatically again: "There!"

I strained, "I can't see anything."

"Well, of course not, dummy. You can't see it from here."

"*It* what?"

"The Wolf's Lair."

"The what?"

"The Worm's Squirm."

"You've got to be daft."

"How about Dragon's Deep?"

"The Dagon's...?"

"The Chief's digs, *idiot!*"

"And just where be these 'digs'? Close by?"

"Not on your dead feet, they aren't. Remember that 'great shadowy complex' you spotted."

I hadn't realized he'd been so observant as we surveyed the city from the lip of the cave. "How did you know...?"

"I don't miss much. That's how I've survived so long around here. I saw you spot it, but better I saw the look on your face, something we call around here *The Deep's Draw* or *The Captivation*?"

"I'm captivated, huh?"

"Oh, you been captivated a long time, fella."

"But how we going to get there through this maze of mucky streets and blind alleys. We could be lost in this warren for months and get no closer than we are now." I could see from Faust's face that I'd grasped our situation spot on.

"True. True. It's dozens of miles and days of travel and the place is barely visible from most of these outer ring barrios, but there is a way and we're on it."

Faust could be cloyingly annoying with his mysterious little statements and he could see I was thoroughly annoyed. "Look: we've been on the way and it's getting better. You'll see."

"I'll see *what?*" I snapped.

15

"That, for instance," He pointed to a dilapidated street sign ahead of us. "Haven't you noticed things have been improving over the last few hours?"

"No."

"That deer track we started out on that led into this barrio – how it grew?"

"Yes. From a cramped alley to a series of single lane medieval-like streets. This street is the first we've been on that two wagons might pass side-by-side! Look, we're just wandering in a maze!"

"No, we're not. We're tracking straight and true toward The Deep."

"How do you know? How can you say that?"

Faust responded with his best smug, wicked grin: "Because I don't have to ask for directions. I read the signs. We're on the way and right where we should be."

"And where's that?"

"The Boulevard."

"The Boulevard?"

"Our Chief's famous Boulevard of the Angel of Light, of course," Faust pointed at the street sign we'd pulled parallel to. It read *ngel of Light* and like the sign I'd seen before it, it had been much abused and broken off. Faust located the other half stuck in the muck some feet away - *The Boulevard of the A* – its gold lettering scratched and gnawed. He carefully placed it against the street post. "Little respect around here for important things," he grimaced, "but that'll change. Indeed, that'll change in a big way. Come along now. Pick up the pace. Things will get better soon."

"Soon" proved to be another twelve hours travel and a stop at another of Faust's safe houses, where I collapsed and slept for another half day. "Better" proved to be the widening of the Boulevard to some three lanes, one of which was cobblestone, rough walking, but at least no muck.

Faust and I began the next leg of our trek as evening grayed and darkened, and as darkness closed in, I noticed bright steady light ahead on our very limited local horizon. "Ha, ha," Faust slapped my shoulder, "there she shines! The Great Bright Way. Now we'll make time."

"The Great Bright Way?" I mumbled.

"Yes! We're outta the sticks and the boonies now and headed for the big time, the fast time. Wait 'til you see it! The Chief's very own creation. The only way to travel."

"You mean this joke," I pointed to the sorry excuse for a pavement we were on, "is 'The Chief's very own creation?'" My tone said it all: I'm underwhelmed and thoroughly under impressed - "OUCH! What's that for!?" - It had gotten me a slap up the back of the head from Faust's grubby palm.

"Disrespect, boy, and for that you should have gotten much worse. Watch yourself."

"Watch yourself!" I growled back. That only earned me a second harder head slap causing me to bite my tongue.

"Look," Faust shook his finger in my face. "The Boulevard may begin like any other highway or byway – a footpath winding down a cliff-face or a cramped walk-way between ancient buildings, but it doesn't stay that way. It transmogrifies into something that puts the old Roman Roads in the shade, puts old Adolf's *autobahns* in limbo and dwarfs old Eisenhower's interstate highway system into insignificance. There's nothing quite like The Boulevard anywhere in the Old World or the New!"

I resisted *Yeah, right-ing* Faust's obvious hyperbole and rather took the *I'll wait and you can show me* route.

Faust carried forward and carried on: "I remember when The Chief first laid out His plans for the Boulevard. He knew how dense and crowded His Megalopolis had become. He saw how we ground up its persistent hills, a slur and drag of traffic, rumble of diesels down the corridors of evening. He saw how lights ran through their meaningless rituals of warning and go. He was the original free-thinking visionary social engineer with no qualms about the direction of His progress. The Chief was expansive, committed to building something worthy of His pride, and so He signed off on the demolition of a quarter of the city and the displacement of millions of souls - far more than that meager three million that the Chinese Communists moved to build their tiny Three Gorges Dam on the Yangtze."

Faust's matter-of-fact tone carried no concern at all for the displaced and what may have become of them, though I'm certain if I asked, I'd simply get the short-hand "relocated" answer. I should have just continued to listen, but it has never quite been my nature, and I had to blurt something foolish: "Didn't some of those souls protest, or at least quietly grumble? I'm sure some must have."

"Well, of course, they did!" Faust laughed. "Protest and grumble? That's our stock-in-trade 'round here. Haven't you noticed? Protest and grumble, *and do what you're told!* They did as they were told. They weren't the point of the Boulevard. The Boulevard was the point of the Boulevard. Faust laughed even harder. "Boy, you need to understand *our* folk. They're unpromising people restless to settle always somewhere new. People of the snip and the tuck, those tight disciplines of youth and beauty. They jog on, men who will always be boys; women who lost their names while Adam slept."

Beyond the drone of Faust's voice, I became aware of the under-hum of thousands of tires and the whiz and whoosh of vehicles cutting through the air at high speed. The light beyond the suburb ahead was sharpening, illuminating our way forward as the roadway became smoother and wider. Faust stopped below a billboard and ordered, "Read. The Chief penned that dedication long before what He calls *His Great Wide Way* was anywhere near finished. It's a real celebration of the thing and no one is permitted to forget it, *not even you.*" Faust ended with a hint of menace. And I? I read!

> Now we'll cruise, acceleration and the passing lane
> quick as the pressures that drive us, fast
> as the laws of chance and accident permit.
> We'll pass the mirrors that buildings have become,
> race down the Avenues of Bald Seductions.
> We'll dream dreams, large volumes of frauds
> and vague fictions, celebrate we're back in style,
> and this is my world and welcome to it.

"A few of those grumbling wags called the Boulevard The Chief's highway-from-nowhere-to-nowhere, but they were swiftly silenced, stupid miscreants who have no understanding of the nature of progress here." Faust fell silent for the next few blocks until we stepped from the shadows of the last row of buildings fronting on the Boulevard into a blazing glare of lights and roar of engines that stunned our senses. I grabbed a railing to prevent myself from being swept into the maelstrom created by the passing of a long line of heavy transports, swept and blown under their tires. Faust shouted into my left ear, "SURPRISED?"

I confess I was, and dazed – and breathless – and nearly blinded by the high intensity highway lighting. "THE BOULEVARD ARROWS EAST, WEST, NORTH, AND SOUTH, AND CIRCLES, LIKE THE JEWELED TIARA IT WAS MEANT TO BE, THE CHIEF'S GREAT COMPOUND!" I shook my head in the affirmative, but stepped aside from Faust for a breath of fresh air. He stepped after me and I was about to wave him back, when he shouted: "LOOK SHARP. HERE'S OUR RIDE!" A stretch limo coasted to our curb, Faust pushed me in, and seated himself beside me. "The Deep, driver," Faust ordered and we were off, the acceleration pressings us momentarily into the soft cushions of the seat.

Finally, I could catch my breath and survey the Boulevard without its stultifying light and sound show, while I rubbed my long walk out of my aching limbs. In the comfort, warmth, and perfumed air of the limo, I could begin of absorb what I could see of the Boulevard as we raced on, and what I saw left me almost speechless. The design was…, was…, yes, there was only one suitable word for it: *megalomaniacal.*

In one way, the design seemed to be an urban planner's dream: the arrow straight corridors of the road with nothing to impede their progress, every transport system precisely placed,· twenty lanes for transports in each direction, the median reserved for power lines and a dozen rail tracks. Mass transit and fast transit. Bullet trains and elevated maglev systems shot by at incredible speeds. Everything and everyone seemed to be rushing everywhere and yet nowhere in particular. I glanced at Faust and my "saucer eyes" must have said it all, because he simply murmured, "I told you so."

"One question?"

"Still?"

"Yes. What happens when something goes wrong?"

"Like what?"

"A transport or a carrier wipes out or there's a derailment."

"You don't want to know!" Faust crowed and laughed at my shock. "Let's just say things get very messy very fast."

Broad was the way, indeed, and bright! Try as I might I could see little out the tinted windows of the limo beyond the limits of the Boulevard. The lights that lined it had the effect of throwing the buildings beyond them into vague shadow and seeing any real distance was impossible. We rocketed past an accident some minutes later and I glimpsed debris scattered over seven lanes – an engine here, an overturned transport there, several mutilated bodies akimbo on the roadway. Our driver astutely maneuvered us around and through the traffic with little slowing or discomfort, but I could now grasp Faust's meaning, when he said things could get messy very fast.

For us, they didn't and an hour later the driver announced over the limo's intercom that we were approaching the great Ring Road of the Boulevard and would soon swing into the tunnel system under The Chief's main compound. As we zoomed onto the inner lane of the ring, I felt the vehicle decelerating and in an instant the bright lights disappeared, replaced by the blue light of the entrance tunnel. We mounted a long ramp that brought us out on the plateau of the compound. Whatever I might select – The Forbidden City in Beijing, Hitler's plans for Germania, the Kremlin, Triumphal Paris – all were unimpressive beside The Chief's Palace Prime – not a palace at all, but a sizeable city of palaces.

I'd noticed that security appeared absent as we entered the tunnel system and mounted the ramp, but as we coasted to a stop, security was everywhere, guards at every entrance, crisp personnel who checked and rechecked identity papers. However, when Faust eased out of the limo, several stood to at attention and a high ranking officer motioned him toward the great entrance hall beyond. I followed sheepishly, worried that at any moment I might be yanked aside and taken away as an unexamined interloper. I caught the officer's deferential "my Lord" to Faust and he padded along as if he were almost at home here. *Amazing*, I thought, thoroughly cowed and giddy with nerves over what lay ahead.

MEETING THE CHIEF AGAIN
FOR THE FIRST TIME

I met him!

"The honor is all mine," He smiled, "Your reputation has long preceded you," *and bowed* as He extended His hand. I nearly passed out from nerves and exhilaration.

I met Him and He wasn't anything like what I imagined, even less like how He's ever been described. I want to capture and covet each and every word He uttered to me. I *knew* Faust was pulling my leg, knew it! "Here," I said to myself, when I was introduced, "here is a personality with acumen, culture; a nature prim and correct, philosophical and penetrating in His outlook. He sees what has to be done and acts without compunction. Why, He's the very height of intellect, the grandest of intelligences. His last words to me, before I was ushered out, said it all: "You'll go far, my man, very far. There's nothing between us. Believe what you like. It's better that way. I can live with that."

What benign understanding and appreciation! What tolerance! I left dazzled. Even Faust's cynical smirk, when I told him about the audience, didn't bring me down. He simply shook his head and knew enough to keep his retorts to himself. Yet, I shouldn't be too hard on Brother Faust. After all, he set things up. Told me The Chief sometimes meets His new recruits, especially those with special promise and I guess I had particularly special promise about me, for when we arrived at the sprawling palace compound, all the guards clicked to attention and marched us in. They were all grace and welcome to me, though I noticed Faust didn't fare as well. Some of the guards in a nearby barracks spotted him and sang out:

> "Fassie, Fassie, he's our man.
> Soon enough he'll be in the jam.
> Fassie, Fassie, under the ban..."

Their chant trailed off as we entered the building before us. Faust had flushed at their disrespect and begun to raise his fingers in an obscene gesture, but he was too slow. They were all ready with their own and ended the show with the two fingered gesture from their eyes to his, which said with unmistakable clearness, "We're watching, Bro. We're watching you." It was the only moment I had misgivings, misgivings swept away instantly as the great bronze doors to The Chief's own chamber eased soundlessly open.

I turned to Faust and motioned him to step in before me as my senior and guardian, but he shook his head and murmured, "No. This is your show, not mine. He never sees me anymore. Likes me, but doesn't trust me. And why should He? Why should He trust anybody?" Faust stepped back into the dark hall and vanished without a sound. I really took in nothing but his "no" at that moment, a moment too momentous for anything more than that passing word.

I was intent on absorbing the moment, to capture its every nuance, and preserve it all. I wanted to remember word-for-word what The Chief said, for His words were the mirror images of my own thoughts. After we were introduced, he adjusted his tweed sport coat and settled into his overstuffed chair. His loafers shown like polished onyx and the warmth He exuded could have heated the room.

"You're the p-perfect image of a sch-scholar," I stuttered.

He chuckled self-deprecatingly: "Yes, I'm a natty dresser, aren't I? But other than the diamond stick pin and gold finger rings, I'm probably far more diminutive than you expected."

He could read the answer on my face – *awe*. No, not diminutive at all. *Overwhelming*.

He was more than a "natty dresser." He was the very image of fashion. His shirts? He wore only pastels with banded collars. His pipe added just the right intellectual touch and sweetened the atmosphere of the room with its aromatic tobacco.

He asked who I liked to read and I blurted, "Why Nietzsche, of course! Who else is there!?"

Yes, who." He rejoined and patted me warmly on the shoulder. "Me perhaps? But, of course, I've written almost nothing and never will. So, you're one of my grateful 'god-is-dead' fans. Wish there were more like you, but we can't expect miracles, can we?"

We both had a laugh at that, but for my part I failed to perceive any humor in His comment. "Yes," he lisped. "Yes, my friend, you're right.

Nietzsche was right: God *is* dead and where does that leave me? *Me,* a widower of sorts you might say."

He smiled mischievously at me and launched forward on what I thought was one of His great insights of the evening: "No, there's no such thing as evil, is there? And I must agree, of course, for I know where that leaves any thought of good. Don't trouble yourself about it. As I said: There's nothing between us. Believe what you like. It's better that way. I can live with that."

He tapped out his pipe and considered me for a long, almost uncomfortably long, moment, uncomfortable because He almost seemed to be sizing me up or down, taking my measure, estimating something. I felt utterly naked, and for a millisecond, like a child under the gaze of a pedophile, but that passed as soon as it came, for then He examined His pipe, glanced up and murmured, "Let's explore what brought you to us. If I'm right, you were one of our most progressive thinkers."

I blushed. Indeed, my reputation had preceded me, but I declined to brag, simply shrugged my shoulders, and blandly smiled. "I tried."

"And try as you might, you certainly succeeded," The Chief motioned me to take a seat opposite him. "You certainly turned some of the world right-side-up for once."

"Some accused me of turning the world upside down."

"No. Definitely not," He leaned forward, wagging a long, manicured finger at me. "You turned our side up and we're grateful for it. That kind of service should not go unrewarded!" What could I do? I veritably glowed, but I knew, even here, I shouldn't take all the credit.

"What was I? One of ten thousands, all pushing the agenda.... I just had good teachers."

The Chief dismissed my mock humility with a knee slapping "HA!" as if I'd made an amusing observation. "You had dolts for teachers, minor minds. In spite of them, you're more like a leader of ten thousands. More like a leader, my boy. As I'm fond of saying, humility just doesn't fit the bill here."

"Yes, sir." I blushed, caught out in my own hypocrisy. I decided to hoe a different row, play up instead of down. "Might I respectfully ask which of my efforts you found most interesting?"

"Indeed you might, my boy, and I'll gladly tell you. Gladly!" Now The Chief glowed, His features exuding deep amber. "It was your call for a whole new basis of law, a jettisoning of that creaking, decrepit old Judeo-Christian foundation, for a cosmic concept based on relativity, individuality, and narcissistic self-interest. That call for a new breed of super-selves, vying for Darwinian dominance: it captured the young minds of a whole generation!"

"Some condemned it as simply super-sizing the ego," I grimaced, remembering how some pilloried my reputation.

"Tosh! Enemy propaganda. You grasped something large, worked to engineer major social change and were recognized by many as one of the great activists of your time." The Chief said more, much more, but the exhilaration of remembering it has exhausted my ability to record it.

Near the close of our little conference, The Chief touched a call-button and smiled: "Now it's time you meet my second-in-command: one Stopheles. You'll find him much to your liking: urbane and dignified on most occasions, highly educated and astute – just the kind of fellow with which I like to surround myself." I beamed. It spoke well of The Chief's astute administration.

~~~~~

Stopheles proved every inch the image The Chief had described. I suppressed a smile at his clothing. Dressed in a black suit, sporting a black tie, he appeared every inch an undertaker, but perhaps that's the way The Chief liked him. Stopheles nodded and offered me a firm, but cool handshake (an undertaker's handshake?), then turned to The Chief: "So this is *him*."

"This is him. Keep him in mind. You'll be seeing a good deal of him," and The Chief turned to me: "*And* you'll be seeing a good deal of Stopheles. You'll find him a truly great instructor."

Before I knew it, the door was closing behind me and I was again in the outer hallway. Audience over. I stood stark still and for a few seconds wondered if the whole experience had been a dream or a fantasy, but then I open my hand and *it* was there. The copper that The Chief had pressed into my palm as I was leaving: "Your pass, if for some reason you need to return." I examined it, turned it over. Yes, it was a copper, about the size of an American penny, well worn and clearly abused by whoever received it before me, but it was now my special possession, my open and unfettered access to The Chief.

I walked out into an evening bathed in torchlight and permeated by the odor of burning garbage. I glanced toward the barracks. The guards had disappeared, though I could hear their distant, muffled guffaws. Faust was nowhere in the courtyard and only when I passed under the heavy portcullis did I find him walking along the moat.

On spotting me, he immediately turned on his heel and walked double time toward the shadowy suburbs below us. I followed meekly, though not quite willingly, a follower again, no longer the honored guest. We spent the night at a dilapidated Inn. I didn't sleep much. The mice in the walls kept me awake and when I began to drop off, a distant shriek or moan or growl would snap me back to full consciousness. Two or three times, someone tried our door and I was particularly thankful Faust had locked and double bolted it. Faust didn't rise until noon when we sat down to watery bowls of onion soup and stale bread.

"Dig in! It's the best we'll get today." He didn't look up from his bowl, slurping away until he finally tilted it up and tossed the last of the liquid down his throat. "We've come down a little, haven't we now!" He wiped his mouth on his frayed and filthy sleeve.

Cheer it wasn't; rather, thick patronizing and I didn't much like it, but I had to confess, after the high of early last evening, meeting The Chief and all, it had all been downhill. I made a study of ignoring his suggestion.

"Shouldn't it be?"

"Not to my mind."

"Not to *his mind*, he says!" Faust's snorted. "What kind of mind is *that*?"

SOUR MILK TO THE *Nth*-POWER

Cynicism has a way of gnawing you down to your bitters. While I struggled to maintain the remains of my euphoria at meeting The Chief, Faust's nagging negativism led to the evaporation of any semblance of good spirits I might have had and with that evaporation the atmosphere here became cloyingly close, oppressive. My days grew heavy, like those occasional days *back before* - those gray, damp, drizzly, dreary days and weeks that beset us at certain times of the year, except here they don't beset us *at certain times*. They seem to beset us all the time - week upon week, month upon month, year after year!

But it's not just the atmosphere. It's the neighbors. They're passive-aggressive, smiling up front, all daggers behind my back. Ask a question – get an accusation. Make a compliment – get a put-down. Say "good afternoon" and in return, someone spits, "And what's your problem!?" That kind of response wearies one out, makes one testy. I snap, when I mean to give a calm reply. I become suspicious of others, even when I've not seen them for some time. I feel like I've contracted the mean accusatory virus that infects everyone here.

Beyond these stupefying "atmospherics" though, stands Faust. Faust the bitter, the rough, the eternally oppositional – or should I say, Faust the terminally infected, always backbiting. If I say "tomāto," yes, he says "tomăto." I find myself edgy, irritable, given to outbursts of anger, even....wrath. And fool that I am – and yes, I confess *now* that I AM a fool – I complained to him of the life that brought me here: my grubbing pursuit of money, dancing with debilitated starlets, sleeping with all the women I could seduce. Yes, I, the stardust child, a wild exploiter of everything and everyone. My divorce, divorces, abandoned sons and neglected daughters by a dozen different women. Every squandered hour at the crap tables in dozens of gin-and-tonic soaked casinos. A 7&7 in one hand, snake eyes in the other, high roller of the low life, web crawler through every pornographic perversion in that sexual Babel of too many chat rooms and webcam voyeurism.

As I inhaled deeply, I caught the dirty little man eying me with more than his usual distaste. "So what's *your* problem? Why did you do it anyway? And don't give me any of that perils of Pauline crap about 'not doing the good you want, but evil you don't want.' None of that 'O what a wretched man, am I! Who will save me from this body of sin and death?!'[2] It doesn't wash here. It definitely doesn't wash!"

Both his attitude and tone were so scathing that I probably said the one thing I shouldn't have around here. With my best sheepish smile, I shrugged and gurgled, "Guess The Chief just made me do it."

"The Chief?" Faust roared. "The Chief?! You lay that on The Chief with everything else He has to carry?! Look you little worm, you wait one hell of a minute! *The Chief made you do it?* Not likely." Faust had darkened considerably and swelled to half again his size, his eyes frog bulging like someone with an extreme thyroid condition. Me? I shrank back, stepped back, backed off in case he exploded with violence, but he stunned me by transmogrifying from avenging angel to the enraged instructor drumming his indoctrination into his miscreant student:

"Whatever it was that turned and bit you, poisoned your life, it wasn't Him! That's a bad rap, bad press, that's all it is, tales told by fools not even brave enough to face themselves. They're liars all, veritable slithers of bad faith, tellers of tales tall and small. I'd never trust their signatures on any contract!" Faust could see my next lame claim rising and crushed it like a cockroach: "And don't tell me you're innocent! Everybody uses that! And don't you dare claim Eve was innocent until The Chief came along! No, she'd been told in no uncertain terms: *Do NOT eat!* Yes, she was warned, amply warned: *Eat and you will surely die!* You can't plead innocent with that kind of information – and from the very source of Truth! Nor was Adam any less guilty, pointing fingers at everyone but himself, the bitter tang of death fresh in his mouth, his breath corrupt as decomposing flesh.

"Look: If you're hungry and try to turn stones to bread, your broken teeth are your own fault. Do a graceless swan dive off the pinnacle expecting to wing it up with the angels and you're to blame for your own shattered body. And how could anyone possibly believe all the kingdoms of this world were The Chief's to give in payment for a simple soul? And yet most fall for that one every time!"[3] Faust's tirade had taken his last breath and left him momentarily speechless, but only momentarily. He sucked in a huge breath and spat out his bottom line, punctuating each word with its own painful jab to my shoulder: "The true liar's the one who buys the lie!" He glared, turned on his heel, and left me violently alone. And me? I crawled off to my hovel to lick my wounds and feel sorry for myself, hoping that he'd not expose me to The Chief.

Later I began to simmer, chewing his denunciations over and over: *I had NOT claimed Eve was innocent!* How could Faust accuse me of that! And how *dare he* defend The Chief! Faust and his "The Chief likes me, but doesn't trust me." Right! Right He shouldn't. Faust is a two-faced, forked-tongue liar. Yet, even as I thought that, I remembered Faust's fondness for quoting Emerson: "Consistency is the hobgoblin of small minds."

No, I muttered to myself, *consistency is the hobgoblin of devious minds.* Yet, Faust's "The true liar's the one who buys the lie," dogged me down my next few days and old Pilate's "What is Truth?" kept pace along side of it. They sang across my synapses like a bad song one can't get out of one's head. Enough to give one headaches! No, *migraines!* I began having migraines.

~~~~~

Faust. How did I come by him? Was he assigned to me or did he just find me out there in the gray void. He's clearly no friend. Not even a guide. More like a cantankerous familiar or a renegade fellow traveler who would betray me in a nanosecond if there was something he could gain from it. The bastard *is* intelligent in a negative sort of way and prides himself as a walking archive of forbidden knowledge. Forbidden knowledge? My eye! *Here?* Where nothing seems forbidden? And yet he insists some things *are.*

Nothing *seems* forbidden, but on second thought, I must confess that even here, we've things that are NOT DISCUSSED, no, not even in the most impolite company. Not discussed, except in the most secret and secluded recesses of this place by those who are either fools or exceptionally suicidal; not discussed in any open way, because to do so would bring down such wrath as to onion-skin us alive, layer-by-layer, until nothing remained.

Yet, even here what dare not be discussed still leaks out and learning the secrets of such a place has its one plus: you at least know where to step and where not to step. However, learning secrets has its unpleasant side, one of them being Faust's breath, sour milk to the *nth*-power. His secrets are best whispered in almost inaudible tones for every shadow seems to contain an ear, every byway a resident spy. So I've tolerated his hot, rancid breath searing my eardrum. "I'll say this only once and that's probably once too often, especially if you ever let it be known that you know. Say one word and you'll be on report. They'll have you dragged in, tortured until you give me up, and then pack both of us off to their ovens for a millennium of roasting."

"They'll? Who's they? And why are you telling me at all?"

I thought he'd say "because I trust you," or "because I like you," but he merely murmured: "because I want to. I like to cut against the grain, flaunt the rules, and break the laws. That's why He likes me, even though He doesn't trust me, doesn't trust me a whit."

I, too, didn't like Faust and even more didn't trust him - a whit. I was with The Chief there! Why was he telling me? Was he building an elaborate trap to capture me in some dubious nether transgression, then serve me victim-side up to The Chief as an accused and guilty traitor, stuck in the sticky web of my own curiosity?

"Look," I exclaimed, "it's better to keep anything to yourself. Understand?"

Apparently not, for he took a hard, lingering look around, searching every shadow, before cupping his hands to my ear: "From what tiny shred of scuttlebutt I've heard, He made the grand miscalculation."

"He? He who?"

"Don't be deaf and dumb: Our Chief, stupid. He risked everything for everything, reached to grasp the vast glittering prize of the universe, but even as He closed His fingers on it, it vanished - it and every solid thing around Him. The celestial floor evaporated under His feet and He heard Michael shout: 'Going down!'"

"Michael? Who's Michael?"

"Michael. You don't want to ever meet him. You don't even want to know anything about him here, least of all his name. So down The Chief fell: fell beyond any one's recollection, fell beyond hope, fell from any last tatter of a possibility of love. He knew it was an exit with no entry, when He dove from that high platform. Sometimes He tucked tight. Sometimes He simply cart-wheeled through the unrelieved dark; sometimes He spread-eagled like a skydiver and heard His huge wings flail and riffle like half-opened parachutes. But mostly He shrieked like a pilot going in nose first, His screams lost, and more than lost in His enemy's silence."

I considered Faust as he inspected the floor, searching for more words or perhaps just little worms with large ears. Was he fibbing me? Was this some test? Or was he playing a sort of blind-man's-bluff, betraying The Chief's intimate secrets, doing the traitor for thrills, risking not only himself, but me in the bargain. I wanted to yell *stop*, but seemed transfixed by his hypnotic stare. In spite of the howls from my inward alarms, I listened.

"In spite of His catastrophic expulsion, I don't think The Chief was really surprised. He knew overreaching could be His grand slip and fall, but His confidence, His arrogance, *His pride* demanded that He risk it. He thought it would either be His grand moment of triumph or conflagration, a quick coup or a interminable war, but in the very second He chose and acted, He realized He didn't have half enough power to stay, let alone stop, the enemy's hosts that drove Him and all of His over those towering escarpments."

My heart drummed at the horror of it, the indescribable terror of an all but infinite fall! I found myself trying to catch my breath, my mind reeling with the vision of it, the over-arching loss, the sweeping defeat, the numbing rush of utter, irreversible failure. But even as I shivered, bathed in cold sweat, Faust whispered on: "Don't let The Chief ever fool you! He knows it's still better to reign *there* than rule *here,* for even though He established *here* what He wanted to establish there, He's never been satisfied with the results and rages against what He calls *the detritus* of His existence."

We sat in silence for several minutes, each of us lost in his own thoughts. I looked at my hands and found them shaking

"You're some kind of renegade, aren't you? Or worse, *a traitor.*" I growled.

Rather than return my anger or denounce my accusations, Faust simply chortled. "Thanks for the compliment." He smiled, but it was a mirthless smile.

"It wasn't a compliment."

"That's what you think," he guffawed. "It is here!"

"Why couldn't you be like Virgil?"

"Never claimed to be. Never wanted to be. He ain't me and me no him. No. Nada."

"Now you're doubly mocking me." Faust merely laughed more.

I decided I wasn't going to let go of the subject. *"Back when,* we always thought of Virgil as the Guide-in-Chief around here. Conveyor, not *purveyor,* of confused souls."

"All because of that Alighieri fella and his infernal *Inferno?"*

"Well, maybe, yes. You know, the noble Roman, the great poet, the consummate student of history, the best of good guides in the earthly sense."

Faust spat over his left shoulder, his special way of showing disdain: "That whole Dante thing was a gross anomaly," a strong undertow of anger entered his tone: "Should have never happened, and worse, he should never have been allowed to report at the end of it all."

THAT NIGHT LIKE NO OTHER

The wonderful thing about paranoia? It helps you find even the enemies you don't really have.

Enough of Faust now. He had planted his seeds of suspicion, and, in spite of my best effort, they sprouted early and grew like noxious weeds. First, he had crushed and destroyed my emotional high over meeting The Chief. Then Faust had planted his little garden of misgivings and falsehoods – but which were legitimate misgivings and which were falsehoods? He'd poisoned my spirit and now, everywhere I looked, *enemies, spies, traitors* – and I increasingly felt he was setting me up for a betrayal worthy of Judas or Brutus or Rasputin or Hitler…. But, how to counter him? That was the question. If his game was betrayal, how could I expose him, before he accused me?

Faust had already told me too much and my very possession of such knowledge might make me suspect, or worse yet, guilty for having listened to it and not reported him. Anyway, what did I owe the dirty little creep. All he'd done was pick me up, dust me off, and lead me through the muck and mire of his personal sewers. Yes, he'd taken me to my meeting with The Chief, but that was, of course, on The Chief's very own direct order. The bottom line was that Faust was nothing to me, but a problem, a danger, a double agent that couldn't be trusted, either by myself or by The Chief.

There was one answer and only one answer: betray Faust, before Faust betrayed me.

~~~~~

Thus it was that I decided I'd had enough of Faust's tender regard. I reasoned that he was not only dangerous to me, but even more so to the state of things here. Though an occasional doubt about my course of action drifted lazily across the vague boundary between my conscious and subconscious selves, I rejected it, knowing that there was One here who was bright and farseeing enough to sort everything out. That may seem a tad bold of me, but I was feeling bold and, anyway, The Chief had received me most positively and seemed to have given me his *imprimatur*.

More, The Chief didn't trust Faust, neither did I, and now I felt I knew why. *Time to consult with The Master and turn Faust in.*

I began to suspect, too, why The Chief and Stopheles had not scheduled another meeting with me. The Chief, Himself, had emphasized that I'd be drawn to return at the proper time and, though at the time I had had no idea what a "proper time" might be, it now dawned on me that they relied on situations like mine to draw me back. I was not being tested. I was being trusted, trusted to hear the dissonance in the voices of supposed loyalists, trusted to see the double lives of double agents bent on undermining The Chief's realm. And, with Faust's increasing disrespect of The Chief, his whispered disloyalties, his tale bearing, I had my work cut out for me.

Day dreams began to tease me as I walked through the streets and alleys on my way to The Chief's Palace Prime and those dreams fortified me, dreams of entering The Chief's chambers again, of being warmly embraced by Him, of our heart-to-heart discussion of "our Faust problem" and what to do about it, and of the rich reward of thankfulness and more I might well receive. By the time I came in view of the compound, I was a decorated hero, a rich and trusted adviser, promoted to one of The Chief's chief lieutenants.

So, imagine my shock, when I raised my eyes to those towering walls and saw – not the vast and soaring city of imperial palaces, not the daunting black battlements of the stronghold I'd seen last time, but something more akin to Nebuchadnezzar's sorry ruins. Dead vegetation hung from the shattered walls. The portcullis of the main gate hung dangerously askew, and neither lamp nor torch relieved the gloom of the place. The entire expanse of the vast compound had been reduced to ramshackle ruins close to collapse.

Dazed, I stepped forward far more slowly, more cautiously, more tentatively – with misgivings that something dreadful was amiss. The moat was at low ebb, a toxic soup rank with red algae and decomposing corpses. The draw bridge was down, but hung askew on one of its great chains. No guards appeared and the place was, well, yes, silent as the old tomb cliché. I was about to turn back, but remembered Brutus' great shout at the Battle of Philippi, that "the tide of events when taken at its full leads on to victory." Problem was, the tide seemed out and victory seemed to be hiding, cowed, among the ruins here. As I crossed the parade ground within the first defense perimeter, I noticed the barracks stood shuttered and dark. Only a rat or two scurried across the open yard and somewhere deep within the pile of buildings ahead of me, I heard a rusty hinge groan, then shriek.

"OK," I murmured to myself, "wrong place? Wrong approach? Wrong time?" Everything seemed wrong. Nothing was like it had been; nothing was like it should be. The place was a chaos, albeit a quiet one. I was considering turning around and beating a hasty, but strategic retreat, when I reached The Chief's personal stronghold, a hold that no longer looked so strong. Its cracked and crumbling walls betrayed their coming disintegration. The Chief's great palace doors stood scorched and smoking from what must have been a recent assault. "Time to hightail it out of here," I whispered to myself and turned to sprint back across the parade ground.

"HOLD THERE!" A huge, hulking form separated itself from the shadows on my left. I stopped all but dead in my tracks. Whatever it was, our immediate surroundings filled with a most unpleasant odor. "HOLD!"

"I'm holding, I'm holding!"

Its huge face – a face covered with scars and lesions and several revolting suppurating growths - came closer to mine. I shrank from both its visage and its cesspit breath, shrank only to be yanked off my feet by its filthy claws at my throat. "*Oh boy...*," I groaned and choked.

"WHAT do you THINK you're doing here, BOY?!" His question exploded in my face along with a reasonable amount of greasy sputum.

Somehow I managed to force enough air through my bruised larynx, to rasp, "Chief...see Chief...."

"Chief ain't seeing no one!"

"Chief...will see me...," I can't believe I got the words up, let alone audibly out. How did I know The Chief would see me! However, the statement did have some effect. The grip on my throat loosened slightly and the Face in my face drew a couple of inches back. Apparently this great hulking menace was uncertain for the first time - but only for a second.

"YOU GOT A SUMMONS THEN," it boomed.

How I would have loved to shout "YES" at that moment, but I was more than a tad short on the summons ledger. "No," I grunted and felt its hold tightening on my throat again.

"YOU GOT TO HAVE A SUMMONS."

I struggled in its grip for a second, but then went limp, realizing that struggle only increased its pressure on my throat and I was in grave danger of passing out. My limpness probably saved me from being yanked in two and cast in separate corners in the next second. "Important business for The Chief," I barely managed to exhale, more as a broken series of gasps, than as clear words.

"NO SUMMONS; NO BUSINESS."

"About *trai-tor*," I gasped, and knew it was about to be my last utterance.

However, those two words caused the grip to relent and the thing considered setting me down. It was as if I'd uttered some magical password it was programmed to accept, but only for a second as it considered me with a look of rank suspicion.

"TRAITOR?"

"Yes. Traitor," For the first time, I could speak without almost expiring.

"SORRY. NOT TONIGHT."

"Even about a traitor?" I was taken aback. I thought that would be Priority One on The Chief's list.

"NOT TONIGHT. COME BACK TOMORROW NIGHT." At that moment, something else stepped from the shadows, far smaller, slim, elegant, and bejeweled, dressed in cloth-of-gold, his features so fine and refined that they had a marked feminine delicacy.

As he came closer, he considered me with a benign smile and, reaching up, touched the giant on its elbow. "Good work, Moloch. Good work. You may go now. I'll take care of this."

Moloch grunted, set me down slowly, a little awkwardly, but with almost a mother's care and gentleness, made a meek squeak, and vanished. I shook myself out, straightened my aching shoulders, and bowed to my liberator. He was Stopheles and he asked mildly, "And now, what business do we have?

"The Chief...."

"No one sees The Chief tonight. No one." The words were delivered with polite mildness, but also with a definiteness that brooked no counter. Even if I used my "traitor-ticket" again, I sensed it would be of no currency with him. However, a new tack seemed in order now that Stopheles was before me.

"Forgive me," I apologized and realized immediately apologizing was the wrong approach.

Stopheles, though, didn't seem offended: "We don't grant forgiveness here. We don't even know what it is. You came with an important concern, I suspect."

"You are quite correct," I strove to match his cultured expression, fearing that any less response would consign me to the rank of ordinary drudge.

"But you've yet to understand that no one sees The Chief without His summons?" Stopheles continued his polite diplomatic tone, but I caught in the unmistakable undertone, the under-message, *you will not see The Chief tonight.*

Now it was my turn to squeak meekly: "I understand now."

"Good. Very good."

"Is The Chief ill?" I sensed the hazard in my query only as the words escaped, but still felt entitled to a little more information, given the state of things here tonight.

"Indisposed." Stopheles was the soul of discretion.

I could only murmur a crestfallen, "*Oh....*"

Stopheles smiled: "You didn't check your calendar."

"I wasn't aware I needed one. They don't seem very useful. Time seems a rather meaningless thing around here. The days all run together like quick silver."

"An apt metaphor," Stopheles patted me on the back as he ushered me into a small waiting area, his delicate hand guiding me to a sagging chair. One of its legs was shorter than the rest and I strained to balance myself on it with what little remained of my dignity after my confrontation with Moloch. "Calendars can be useful, though, on occasion, like tonight."

"Tonight?"

"Yes. It's not The Chief's night. You've perhaps noticed the difference?" A polite, but very definite query and I knew I'd better answer it accurately.

"Yes. Things seemed quite different tonight."

"As they always are," Stopheles rejoined and then he began pointing out things I'd missed: how dim and green the lights burned tonight; how the moon was full as a woman with child. "You see, it's Passover once again, isn't it?" *Passover?* Now there's a day I never tracked on. Passover?! I hadn't a clue what an ancient Jewish religious festival might have to do with tonight or a place like this. Stopheles saw my confusion and continued, but seemed to concentrate on his palms, rather than speaking directly to me: "The Chief's in a blue funk and will see no one, not even me." He looked up and caught my surprise at that confession. "Yes, now, perhaps you need a little reading!" He brightened, reached for a small tattered chapbook lying on one of the lowest of his bookshelves. "Here. A little bedtime reading, if you're having trouble sleeping, as most do 'round here. It might help you understand – you know." Stopheles nodded to the left, at what might be the doors to The Chief's chambers for all I knew.

I nodded, taking the handful of pages as if they held the very secrets of creation.

"They don't," Stopheles smiled as if he'd read my mind. "Just some things everyone here learns sooner or later. Better sooner for you." After a few departing words, he ushered me from his presence and closed his door almost soundlessly behind my back. In the dim and wavering light, I considered the well fingered and thumbed cover in my hands. The title it bore, in heavy Gothic, read *The Satanic Sorrows*. I riffled through its pages, closed it, and then opened it again at random, only to see the words that Stopheles had just spoken:

> The Chief's in a blue funk and will see no one.
> He sulks on nights like this about what might
> have been, how if He were Cain,
> He wouldn't have stopped at Abel.
>
> If Solomon, He'd have taught both
> those women a real lesson, divided

their baby between them and left it at that.
As Judas, He'd have gloried in His coins,
but He'd have far more of them than thirty.
Betrayal's a fine and delicate art
and deserves to be very well rewarded!

And if Pilate, He wouldn't even have stopped
to wash His hands, but hurried off to lift
the jug with Antipas and Caiaphas,

and they'd all sing at the top of their lungs.
But it didn't go that way, *did it?*
And that's what galls Him.

And that's what galls Him.

~~~~~

Let me emphasize here: my meeting with Stopheles was almost as precious as the one I had with The Chief, in spite of the obvious run-in with Moloch. The meeting with The Chief had been somewhat *pro forma,* one of those official audiences with important persons for the purpose of introduction. Don't misunderstand me. It was immensely gratifying and stimulating. My time with Stopheles was different: it left me feeling I'd a clear friend very highly placed, someone who understood me and my concerns. When we parted, he shook my hand thoroughly and vigorously and patted me on the shoulder: "Be sure to come again and see me. Use your copper, your pass, the next time to pass through the guards." He pressed something cool into my palm, a second dull copper, as if I'd perhaps thoughtlessly lost my first.

I nodded with a broad smile and said softly, "I am your servant, sir."

Stopheles grinned back and quietly observed: "And more as well I know." Then just before he dismissed me, he leaned forward and whispered intimately, "You need to return *soon.* You need to learn something more, if you are to serve The Chief well against His many enemies."

Euphoric from that invitation, I left the hall, the whole dilapidated compound of palaces and their smashed fortifications, and stepped smartly across the great parade ground, headed down the long road to the city. That's when I became aware of a lingering figure on the path ahead – a short, somewhat stocky, stooped figure. The one man I had no wish to see at the moment, if ever again. I stopped stark still and considered quick-stepping into a roadside thicket, but he'd spotted me and stepped in my direction. I considered turning back the way I'd come, but that would only confirm I was up to no good toward him. Worse, I could hardly return to The Chief's lair. What was I to do? Dance back in on Stopheles crying, "I'm baaackk?"

Faust stopped a few feet away and scanned me head to toe. "Been to see The Chief, I see." He reeked of rank suspicion.

"No, I haven't been." I was beginning to understand what it meant to lie with the truth.

"Indeed, you haven't. It's Passover. Who *did* you see?"

"Stopheles," Faust's questions forewarned me I couldn't go too far out on a limb with lies. I decided to stick as close to the truth as possible to make more plausible any falsehood I might be forced to offer him.

Faust's response took me completely by surprise: "Ai-yai-yai! Oh, boy. Ol' Stopheles and he reeled you in without so much as a hook and a struggle!"

"He did no such thing!" I was indignant and kicked myself inwardly from being diverted from my intent to turn the traitor in, even if it was Stopheles who diverted me.

Faust thrust his hands in his pockets and considered his toes. "You went to betray me, didn't you?"

I wrapped myself deeper in my indignation: "Now why in the world would I do *that*?"

"I think we both know."

"I think we don't." My retorts bordered on the ridiculous and shouted the obvious "yes" to his question, but to my surprise – as I braced for some dark and violent move on his part – he changed topics, apparently satisfied he'd achieved the answer he sought.

"Stopheles, huh?"

"Yes. What of it?!"

"You poor, dumb, stupid moron, that's what. And he gave you homework, I see." He nodded at the pages curling in my hand. "Well, better get to it and the sooner the better. Then maybe you'll begin to understand how this place works." He turned and walked briskly away.

I stood rooted in place gazing in the direction he'd taken, finally muttering to myself, "that poor, dumb, stupid bastard." Problem was that his appearance and demeanor, his brief pointed interrogation and curt denunciation, had robbed me of the rosy mood I'd carried away from my time with Stopheles. The sneak had brought me down again!

Finally, I put myself in motion again and breathed to myself: "No problem. Just gives me one more reason to see Stopheles sooner than later, something to look forward to that Faust, lost in his little phantom world of lies, distrust, and betrayal, doesn't have."

HOW THE CHIEF TEMPTED ISRAEL
TO BACK TRACK

I felt the definite tug of a reckoning, a drawing toward betrayal a fortnight later. Faust had not shown himself, had apparently gone into hiding, having sensed my intentions. I'd waited for a time to see if he resurfaced, but his disappearance spoke volumes. He seemed as much on the "outs" at the palace as I was "in," and that made me feel powerful and less worried about any damage he might do me.

I climbed the stiff rise to The Chief's palatial compound once more, one of my two simple coppers in hand. I had no desire to be waylaid by Moloch or his ilk a second time and now put my embryonic trust in my Chief's foresight and pass. As I approached within sight of the ramparts and forward towers, I stopped in my tracks, amazed at the facelift the place had undergone since Passover: no shattered defense works, no piles of broken masonry and defaced palaces. More, the whole immense compound was a dark hive of activity. Guards challenged me at every step, at the refurbished drawbridge, under the restored portcullis, as I entered the great parade ground and later the forward courtyard. The barracks glowed red and resounded with ribald hilarity and raucous shouting, mixed with shrill female laughter. Two or three of the guards sitting on the barracks' steps gave me their *we've-got-our-eyes-on-you* signal, but, unlike Faust before me, I received no obscene gestures or verbal abuse.

At each station, I flashed my coin and the guards clicked their heels, saluted, and motioned me onward. Several gave me a glance of uncommon respect and I squared my shoulders. Only one, as I neared Stopheles' chamber, seemed to snicker and elbow his companion, who snorted and ignored both me and my coin.

Stopheles greeted me politely, if not warmly. I noticed, immediately, the change in his attire – no funereal clothing of our first acquaintance nor the remarkably flashy cloth-of-gold robes on our brief Passover meeting. Tonight he seemed more austere, a tad stiff in a crisp dark pin-stripe business suit. He looked every slim inch the polished, carefully manicured and impeccably groomed executive. We stood before shelves upon shelves, floor to ceiling, of an extraordinary library. I fingered a gold stamped, leather bound set of *The Works of Voltaire,* a richly illustrated *Complete Works of the Marquis de Sade, Lady Chatterly's Lover,* both well-worn and missing several of the most lurid sections. *The Last Temptation of Christ! The Da Vinci Code!* A vast media collection ("Every pornographic site on the Internet – worldwide," Stopheles smirked).

I could hardly take it all in, but did see the collection held no Nietzsche, someone for whom I always looked. "No Philosophy?" It was my hooded way of inquiring.

"Oh, yes, that section's on a lower level – Nietzsche, Marx, Engels, Stalin, Mao, Hitler, Singer, Sanger, all the issues of *The Advocate,* first editions of *Mein Kamp* and *Das Capital* – we've everything. Nothing gets in here without The Chief's *imprimatur.*"

"Indeed!" I was overwhelmed with admiration, both for The Chief and of Stopheles. Intellectual powerhouses of the first rank. Faust was a pygmy in comparison and I.... Well, at least I could pride myself in having been admitted to the right and highest circle. "Utterly remarkable." I beamed at Stopheles, but Stopheles....

He wasn't beaming. He was considering me, his head to one side, his face one of total impassivity, his fist under his chin. I could only liken his look to that of a Pathologist I once witnessed as he decided where to make the first incision. That look was enough to infect one with anxiety and I felt a sudden surge of nausea, just as Stopheles smiled – not quite as warmly as during our first meeting, but at least he smiled! "I'm sorry. Didn't mean to overwhelm you with our library. We've other treasures here, enough to rival and counter the best of the Vatican museums."

"Utterly remarkable. Amazing," I gushed, but I meant it too.

He led me into a vaulted room with a vast mosaic on its floor. It crawled with the clawing figures of a thousand Hebrew slaves, trapped in the hot, stifling, shifting sands of the desert. Some had expired. Others were gasping out their final agony and over it all a vast dark figure spread his shadow. "A very famous work," Stopheles uttered with a quiet reverence, *"Death in the Negev."*

"Who were the artists?" I stood transfixed by the scene at my feet, a horrified slave staring into the vacant eyes of a mummified companion. My nerves crawled with misgiving.

"Ah! Some of the same slaves who made the journey!"

"Do tell!"

"The Chief commissioned it in honor of all those Hebrew slaves He tempted to back track. It – the temptation, not the mosaic – was a brilliant piece of work, The Chief at his best. Would that it had fooled all of them, not just these idiots – and left that raging mad man Moses lost on Sinai without a hand to help him! You know he murdered a man. Some useful Egyptian wretch who was just doing his job, seeing a nasty Hebrew got the beating he deserved."

"So I've heard, but I never heard much about any back tracking."

"Indeed, you wouldn't have. To the conqueror goes the right to write the history, isn't that true?"

"Of course it is," I nodded, sounding like the soul of authority on the writing of history. "I, myself, tried my hand at some articles denying the Holocaust, but got fined and nearly jailed by – the conquerors, you might say."

Stopheles considered the mosaic at some length, then, "The evidence of the back-tracking is there, even in the conqueror's text – you know, the forty years of wilderness wandering, two generations lost when they rebelled and deserted their leader. Neither Moses nor the enemy let them go free and unpunished."

"But The Chief drew lots of them back, those crazy Hebrew slaves, I wager."

"It wasn't even a gamble. It took years, but The Chief can be patient when He needs to be. We could see He was concerned about what was happening, helped to harden Rameses the Second, but Moses checked The Chief at every move, so like a shrewd leader The Chief altered and adapted His strategy, joined the straggling slaves. Imagine it! Himself, mind you, in that beaten, desperate, stinking mass of humanity. When the going got *brutal* and the years dragged them across the sands and all the miracles seemed to have vanished like so many frauds, The Chief began His whispering campaign, spotting each wavering soul and injecting it with a good dose of disillusionment and pessimism, followed by a chaser of false hope, and then capped with soul-smothering despair. Look here! We've immortalized His remarkable temptation at the very center of the mosaic."

Indeed they had! The very letters seems to shift and shimmer in the desert heat, purple on what appeared to be the burnt yellow of sand. It was sand! The toe of my right shoe accidently strayed over the edge of the mosaic. *Packed, hot sand.*

Look how the morning lies hot
and dead upon this land, more oppressive
than slavery. You've gone further than

you ever planned to go: this unpromising
promised land full of dark and bearded men
quick as javelins and equally direct.

Come: you can ease back past Jericho,
past the ruins of Sodom (they're rebuilding
you know, *have sex with us* their old refrain);

bypass the Wilderness – *No Moses, please* –
as if you needed *him* to survive! Come
back to Egypt, where life's at least as square

as a brick, with simple meals and old gods
not too difficult to please. Pharoah not
anywhere as stern as Moses. Perhaps

old Rameses will ask you to pass on, each step
bringing you closer to that ancient,
faceless chaos, over which no god moves

contemplating his endless possibilities.

I carried the vision of the mosaic back to my hovel and spent a
sweaty night, punctuated by moments of exhaustion and waves of
anxiety. Faust's "you poor, dumb, stupid moron" danced in and out of
my consciousness and mixed with Stopheles' retelling of The Chief's
grand temptation. And when I approached the barbed borders of sleep,
one nightmare image after another drifted in and out of focus: a dying
mother with twins clutching at her breasts, a babe inspecting an adder's
hole, two naked emaciated skeletons sifting into the sand.

I was nearly deranged by the morning and, if Faust had crossed my
path, I'd have slain him with a single powerful blow. Faust! In those
moments with Stopheles, I'd completely forgotten the real purpose of my
visit: to betray Faust! Incredible! Stupid! I spent hours berating myself,

fretting again what it would mean if Faust turned on me first. I imagined Stopheles shaking his head in disillusioned disappointment, asking, "After all we did for you, why, why did you not turn the traitor in!?"

Sleep finally came in spite of the muggy heat of day and I awoke several hours later, not refreshed and restored, but at least in my right mind. Stopheles had taken my simple copper from me as I departed, but palmed something somewhat bigger, heavier, in its place. I dug through my sack for what he termed a new and better pass, this one a bronze with a bas relief of a leering, comic face thrusting a vast tongue out of its mouth. I stared at it for hours over the next few days, as if it was telling me something I should know, but I was too dense to conceive what message, if any, it might carry. Likewise, for reasons I was unable to fathom, I had only the most meager desire to seek a third meeting with Stopheles, though it was clear he expected me to visit and even more regularly. "Son," he murmured, patting my cheek, "we need to move you forward with more focus and energy now. Your commencement isn't that far off and we've a great deal of preparation to do between now and then."

I nodded blandly, not quite absorbing his words as to what my commencement might be, simply aware he had called me "son." Son! The more I considered that word, the more my stupor lifted.

Yet, it took several fortnights before my first exhilarating memories of meeting The Chief and then Stopheles began to reassert themselves and slowly draw me back for another visit. I'd not seen Faust since our last meeting on the path down to the city, nor did I care to spend another second's thought on him. We'd become dangerous to one another and I was certain if we met many more times, one of us would destroy the other, either by betrayal or violence.

At least Faust's disappearance, indeed his utter absence, gave me more than a modicum of comfort. Apparently, he was *persona non grata* at the compound and rarely dared show his face. That meant I was in far less danger than I'd feared and it gave me greater room to maneuver, to plot his exposure and betrayal. I examined my new bronze coin again, flipped it in the air, caught it, and whispered to the mocking face in my palm: "Yes, Faust, mock on, mock on while you can. Your days and nights here are numbered and I'll be your match."

HOW FAMILIAR YOU ARE:
LET ME COUNT THE WAYS

Weeks have passed since my meeting with Stopheles, weeks of vegging, weeks without the annoyance of Faust, "free weeks" I might even term them, except for Babylonia's ever-oppressive atmospherics. My readiness to expose Faust and accuse him had been ebbing of late, simply worn away by time and the draining of any sense of threat I felt from him.

Yes, weeks passed. Half the time I've laid on my stained and worn out mattress groaning with migraines, while the other half was spent in furtive forays for food and drink – mostly drink – these runs long after twilight. Open daylight, really simply a lighter gray, than the darkening gray of twilight, had not seemed friendly to me, given irascible neighbors, and likely too my distaste to have anything to do with such common, low-life, peasant types as crawled these streets. I chose midnight as my time and lurked in the shadows of the district. The invisibility of darkness gave me a further sense of superiority, an edge, a feeling of dominance over any who might plot me harm, for I owned the night by my stealth.

Invisibility and anonymity also allowed me to gather intelligence (as it were) on the larger scene around me, though what I heard was somewhat disconcerting - mumbled fragmentary conversations concerning "press gangs" – yes, press gangs, similar to those old fashioned 18th century military "recruiters" that swept the slums and impressed stray souls into His Majesty's service. Something grim was obviously going on, because, for the last couple of weeks, the district streets and alleys had been all but deserted. However, in the last days snatches of whispered news intimated the gangs had moved on to other districts. The heavy tension in the streets had ebbed and a few more souls drifted into the lanes and shadowed about the alleys. Don't get me wrong. No one was dancing in the streets or igniting fireworks. My so-called neighbors still slouched through the darkness, heads down, faces grim. Few stopped to talk with one another and then in groups of only two or three. More, some warned, would attract too much "official attention and concern."

At least with the gangs gone, we'd be able to get out, stretch our limbs, and be about our stunted business of surviving. When I headed back to my room as dawn began to lend the first and faintest of gray to the horizon, I walked with a bounce in my step and a lighter demeanor, not really alert to my surroundings. It had been a particularly profitable foray: I'd snatched a bottle of volka, snitched an armload of bagets, and expropriated some limp, but still edible vegetables, so I didn't spot the bulk of an officer as he stepped from the shadows to my right.

"You! HALT!" My vegetables and bagets plopped to the ground and I lost my grasp on the vodka, which slid from my hand and shattered on the pavement with a sickening 'pop.'

"DON'T MOVE A MUSCLE!"

I stood stark dead and trembling in my tracks. That was better than being dropped stiff and dead in my tracks.

The officer checked my little debris field with the toe of his boot: "Too bad that."

"Yeah." Yes, I was scared, but also annoyed at the extent of my loss, especially the vodka, and I couldn't quite keep the tone of that annoyance out of my voice, something the guard duly noted.

"PAPERS!" He snapped.

I fumbled in my rags and pulled out my identity cards. He inspected them closely and at length, checked the numbers on his com-link, considered me at some length, and clipped: "A fine specimen like you should be in the Defense Forces. Why aren't you?"

"I wasn't asked." Forewarned by murmured gossip, I had proved adroit in avoiding each and every marauding gang until now, but now I cursed my incredible carelessness and my snide tongue. Of course, I wasn't about to confess *that*. Even my rather low key but still cheeky retort didn't go over well and I began to fear I might get the officer's baton across my lips. The only thing in my favor was that he seemed to be a lone wolf, perhaps one of the bounty hunters who traveled in the wake of the gangs, scooping up a few extra souls the gangs had missed.

"Don't be smart, idiot! No more guff or it'll get you a good, smart beating."

"Yes, sir!"

"Are you carrying anything else?"

"No, sir. Not since I dropped everything, sir." Then I remembered my coin and reversed myself, "Well, yes sir, just this, sir."

I fished out and handed him my bronze "mocking" coin. He inspected it closely by electric torch, turned it over several times, as if he expected several more sides or secrets to it to appear. To my relief, he smirked. "Clown pass. Uh huh." He flipped the coin back to me, "Get on home, *clown!*" His smirk lingered as if he knew much more about the significance of the coin than I did, but then as he turned away I heard him mutter to someone in the shadows, a partner I'd not realized was there: "Won't be seeing *him* around here much longer." The other one snorted.

With my recent largess tramped in the dirt, I staggered off around the corner. What were they talking about? How could they know they wouldn't be seeing me much longer? Did they know of orders to pick me up? But no, they'd had me and let me go. *The pass.* Did it indicate some fate? Was I marked for something? Was I simply being promoted or demoted – given a better room, perhaps, in some better district? My mind tripped on at feverish speed.

I now stepped on quickly, turning one corner, then another, stopping to rest in one of the darker alleyways. Then, I stepped out and hurried along the shadows of a side street, headed back toward my room, when someone's fist gripped my collar, yanked me into a doorway, and clapped a second filthy hand over my mouth. "Ssshhhh!" The hot hiss in my ear made me wince, but the cloying corruption of its breath identified my assailant.

"'aus'!" I gagged.

"Shut up," he shook me and growled like a Rottweiler and I went limp in acknowledgment, expecting I was a goner, a pig about to be stuck with a knife in my ribs or a razor across my throat, but as soon as he was sure I'd be quiet, he released his grip.

"*What in The Chief's name are you doing?*" I whispered almost inaudibly.

His breath again nearly overpowered me, but I managed to grasp what was important. "This area's crawling with agents and a half dozen of them broke down your door tonight looking for you. Turned the place over and nearly took *me* away before they realized I wasn't you. 'Let the decadent little devil go,' their leader barked, once they'd confirmed my papers." Faust caught his own fetid breath and then warned: "You can't go back there. The place is a shambles...."

"In case you hadn't noticed," I retorted, "the place was always a shambles."

"Shut up and listen! They could be watching the place or could raid it again. No telling what's up. The whole district's teeming with officers, uniformed and plain clothes and they've got a squadron of security vans just out of sight."

"But I *have* to go back – there's something I need to retrieve."

"Like *what? Your head?*" Faust belched in my face.

"Something only important to me. Something I can't, I dare not, leave behind."

He stared at me as if I was cockeyed and growled: "Nobody here has anything like that." I could see I'd only ignited suspicions that I dearly wanted to avoid. My stomach turned nervously and I began to perspire despite the night chill that pressed in upon us. One thing panicked me: that, if security took the place apart, they'd find the micro-recorder I'd squirreled away between the walls. I knew one didn't record key conversations in Babylonia, unless one had the most seriously suspect and devious motives, but old habits die hard. I'd secretly recorded and exploited everyone all of my life, anyone I needed to control: my wives, enemies, and associates.

I knew Security had found nothing yet or Faust and I wouldn't be standing here, for what was on that recorder would have damned us both: my meeting with The Chief and Stopheles, my conversations with Faust. Faust would already have disappeared without a trace and I'd be on Babylonia's most wanted list, to be hauled in, skewered, and pierced soon as found. My coin wouldn't save me a second time.

"Look. I'm going back. Just forget it and leave me alone, or come along and watch my back." My firmness warned him off. He regarded me suspiciously for another moment, then relented.

"OK. We'll risk it. They've just left and we might have a moment's opportunity before they put the place under continual surveillance."

~~~~~

While Faust stood watch, I mounted the stairs to my room three steps at a time. The door stood open, kicked askew on its hinges. I dashed in, went to the left side of the window frame and worked the left board of the casement loose. The micro-recorder lay in a dark slot behind it. I picked up the wafer thin device, held it to my ear long enough to hear a few muted words, sighed with relief, and slipped the tiny device into my coat lining. The whole scramble had taken me less than two minutes. I dashed back down stairs, and catapulted into the lane.

As Faust stepped from the shadows, I hissed, "Let's go. We've almost completely lost the darkness." Then it hit me! Go where? I realized I'd no place to go. The room I'd just left had been my only bolt hole, my hide-out, such as it was.

Faust read my look and snorted, "Follow me. I've got a couple of safe rooms not too far from here."

"*Safe* rooms? Like those dubious safe houses you used coming into the city?"

"These be safer."

"Right."

"You'll see. Just keep up with me." I was breathless in a few minutes from both the moment's stress and keeping up with Faust's surprisingly fast pace, very surprising for someone who always appeared at the point of physical collapse.

The dawn was expanding across the horizon as Faust slipped down a narrow walkway – one that was almost a claustrophobic squeeze between two dilapidated buildings. He disappeared into a low doorway on the left. "Come on! Come on!" He ordered me, "Get out of the open." Instead of upstairs, we headed down two levels to a bolted steel door. Faust fished up a key, inserted and turned it. The bolt ground back. With a stiff push from his shoulder and a shriek from the door, we were inside.

Pitch dark. No candles here. Faust threw a switch and the entire place was aglow with yellow light. "Electricity!" I exclaimed, then felt embarrassed at my amazement.

"Something like that."

"How…?"

"Don't ask," he growled and there was enough menace in it to shut me up. I surveyed the room – carpet! No dirt floor here. Easy chairs, sofas, and doors leading elsewhere. "Door on the left is for a quick escape, if we need it. The two on the right are sleeping rooms." Sleeping rooms! This place was a mansion in minor key. I was twice as tempted as usual to pursue my questions, but bit my tongue hard, knowing I'd likely get nowhere with Faust.

"No windows," I observed.

"No exterior light, no spies, no surprises." Faust slumped in an easy chair to catch his breath and I collapsed on a sofa, feeling my heart still trip-hammering away. It was only now, after my surprise confrontation with security and Faust, my breathless dash to escape, that the utter irony of my situation dawned upon me. Faust my enemy, Faust my supposed betrayer, had risked his life to save me. I shook my head as if none of the recent events – the meetings with Stopheles, the press gang, even the return of Faust – fit into any rational pattern.

"Maybe an irrational pattern," croaked Faust with his signature smirk.

"Maybe an irrational pattern," I whispered to myself, then threw a surprised, somewhat violated, look at Faust. *What was I? An open book that everyone could read?!*

"No," Faust considered his crabbed hands, "not everyone. Just some of us are less illiterate than others." He chuckled at his own joke.

"Why should you help me?"

"It's my job."

"Help me? The one who was hell-bent to betray you to Stopheles and The Chief?"

"Yep. Anyway you didn't succeed, didn't even come close, did you?"

All I could do was grunt assent.

"Ha, ha!" Faust slapped his bow-legged thighs and laughed until tears began to trickle down his dirty cheeks. He smudged them away: "Sorry to disabuse you, but you're not much at betrayal. You'll never even make the minor leagues. You can't even follow your arse to the toilet!" He beamed with delight at his metaphor.

That stopped me stark dead still. I could only glare at him. "What are you? My leader? Am I Indian to your Chief? Lead on O Great Leader, but your follower has no intention of following."

"Hell no! I'm not your leader! There's only one Chief here and none dare cross Him. You're not expected to follow me, but you damned well sure better follow Him."

"Then you're His servant, or, maybe even better, *mine*." I confess I said that as a nasty little jest, a small vengeful jab. I wanted to needle Faust most pointedly in retaliation for his constant, unrelieved rudeness.

"No! Not *your* servant." The emphasis on the *your* made me think *servant* was somehow still descriptive, and – considering Faust's crabbed and bent ways – another word suggested itself to me: *Servile.* Yes, servile, but certainly not to me

"OK, OK! You're not my guide, my helper, my Vir...." I bit my tongue, biting off the name, before Faust could flare (he was already flushing), "not my servant, thank G...!" I gagged on the word and bit my tongue again.

Faust sneered and muttered as he turned his back and spoke as if to some unseen wraith: "Well, at least he's learning. Hardly an apt pupil, though." He spit a chew of tobacco into a rancid fruit can. "Down right stupid, but that's all we seem to get here."

I think we both decided it was best to proceed in silence for a time, though after a few minutes, I attempted to rise and go to one of the two rooms, to escape Faust's staring presence. I only succeeded in slumping back on the sofa, felled by a wave of lightheadedness. Clearly, I'd run out of energy, too long without even the crudest food and drink.

Faust shook his head as if in assent and muttered, "Grub." He crossed to a table with a burner on it, opened and slammed several cupboard doors, and soon had something concocted. In another few minutes, the burner glowed alive and he slapped a pan on it to heat. I hoped he was preparing it for the both of us, because my recent days and adventures had been passed on the emptiest of stomachs. I decided to break silence, but head our exchange in another direction.

"Then what?"

"What?"

"Then what *are* you."

Faust crabbed over to me, bent down, his face inches from mine, his inflamed eyes locked on mine, the stench of his breath choking mine off: "Little ol' me? Why I'm your very own personal familiar!"

"Familiar?" I hadn't expected that answer.

"Yes, I've been familiar with you for a good many years, my man."

"Familiar? Familiar how? Familiar what?" He wasn't communicating or I wasn't receiving it.

Annoyed, Faust belched: "Whadaya trying to say? *You need a definition?* Now how am I familiar?" He tapped his chin and gazed up at the ceiling in a state of mock thought. "Let me count the ways."

"Well, yes! Who wouldn't need a definition with someone as obtuse as you?" I shot back, irritated by his unbroken rudeness.

Faust ignored my intended barb and announced in his most professorial tone: "Definition number one: *Familiar* as in *encountered* or *seen?*" He volleyed.

"When did I ever encounter you? I never saw you before now!"

"You'd be surprised! A hundred times a thousand we've been face-to-face. Take our most recent travels together: you didn't catch me once as you traveled back and forth to The Chief's digs and Stopheles' chambers!" He flashed a wicked grin – broken, crooked, twisted, but still enough of a grin for me to grimace back.

"Don't be stupid! Nobody could mistake seeing that dirty screwed up mug of yours. This is crazy!" Now I was in his face, really for the first time. "O, the hell with you!"

That oddly seemed to delight him. "Well, we're beginning to get somewhere." Faust broadened his grin adding fuel to my anger.

"Damn it!" I pounded the table to my right, an abandoned glass of stale beer toppling over. "Damn it! Now look what you made me do?!"

"I made you do it? Me? Oh, my!" He literally danced a jig back to his stove with its pan of bubbling liquid.

"Now look! Say what you mean!"

"And mean what I say? I always do," he smirked. "What Faust knows, Faust knows. What you know is what Faust wants you to know." A long silence again hardened between us and I hardened even more as I fretted and steamed, but couldn't find further words with which either to force him to make sense or to assault him. He tasted his stew, smacked his lips, added enough spice to cause a culinary conflagration, finally turned back to me, the wide broken smile, that distortion of a grin, large on his face. "OK! Let me say what I mean: *familiar.*"

"*Encountered* or *seen*, neither of which pertains," I vowed to match him mock for mock, irony for irony, sarcasm for sarcasm.

"Have it your way." He acquiesced too easily. "Definition number two: *Familiar* as in *intimate.*"

"Inti…?!" I recovered enough to stammer, "*You've* been *intimate* with *me*? I think not! Never! Nada! NO!"

Faust smiled, croaking with a cloying coyness: "I *presume* too much? Am I taking *undue liberties*? Am I getting *too familiar*?" He paused, but I found no answer. "Have you never presumed too much? Taken undue liberties? Gotten far, far too familiar, especially – but not only with – the ladies so-called?"

"None of your damned business!" He'd weaseled himself far too close to where I lived.

"But it is my damned business. I'm your familiar, like it or not."

"NOT!"

"Neither here nor there."

"You're an animal," I pouted.

"Ah! An apt pupil for once: discovers definition number four on his own: *familiar: an attendant Spirit often assuming animal form,* then? Sit down. Grub's ready." Faust spun a large bowl of the boiling, noxious stuff across the table. It stopped just short of toppling into my lap. I shoved it back from the edge, burning my fingers, forced to suck the pain from them for several minutes.

"You're an animal, I'll grant that!"

"You're an animal, I'm an animal. 'We're all just a herd of wild, rutting animals. Even when we pray we're simply barking and baying at the moon,' right? Didn't you, yourself, say that far more than once or thrice?" He chortled to himself as he sat down and dipped into his stew, slurping, smacking his lips at it, raising the bowl to his lips and sucking its contents noisily down. I stared, my mind running riot around how he could have known one of my most coveted little quips. He'd reduced me to a lame silence and I turned to my stew and started choking down the searing mess to cover my discomfiture.

Finally, I took a deep breath. "Let's drop the topic, shall we?"

"*Au contraire*! We're just getting familiar," Faust grinned and shoved his bowl aside.

"Case closed!" I returned with high curtness.

"Well, sputter me blubber, no. Not quite yet. There's always that one lingering, little used, old fashion meaning: *Familiar - one who performs domestic service in the household of a high official.*"

"Yeah, right. Aren't you archaic? You're not my servant. You've said so yourself. And you certainly don't look like a high official. And me? I wouldn't be caught dead performing domestic service for anyone, high or low, and especially not for you!"

"Have it your way, but the truth is: I'm still your familiar and I've been that for years and years."

I stared at the table's surface, its chaos of cuts, scratches, and gouges. *Faust* had been carved into the top several times, each time with slightly different lettering – cuneiform, gothic, runes, a mock form of Arabic script. I ran my fingers absently across the deep gouges and confess I was at a complete loss for a come-back. Faust snorted and began to clear the table like the sloppiest of servants.

After singing several little obscene ditties to himself, he turned to me, winked, and ordered: "Sleepy time: Use the sofa, if you like, or the cot in your room there."

"Where you going?" I was disconcerted about being left alone.

"None of your business. All you need to know is to stay put and wait for me to come back. Don't be so familiar." He slammed the door.

I slumped into sullenness and silence, a brooding that lasted the entire day, though it was hard to number the hours in Faust's new bunker-burrow.

YOU BEGIN TO FEEL AS OLD AS METHUSELAH

Faust tried to enter our bunker without making a sound, but the grind of the bolt lock failed him by alerting me and I rolled over blinking at him. "Oh, it's you. Back so soon."

As contrary as ever, he mimicked my "Back so soon," and added "I've been gone all day and half the night, dummy."

"No one followed you back, did they?" I could rise to the occasion at times and ignore his rudeness.

"Nothing but my own stink," he grunted, rolled onto one of our sofas and fell soundly asleep in seconds.

"Nothing but his own stink, he says, which, of course, always precedes him," I muttered to myself and dozed off again. Hours later, we were up at our small table, staring at our empty plates. I'd unwrapped the remainder of our dry and meager rations, barely enough for one of us, definitely not enough for both. We crunched and munched away in silence, sunk in our own thoughts. Food shortages were not uncommon in the city, they weren't even the *new normal* – just the regular, ordinary, everyday grinding old normal. *Abnormal is normal here*, was one of Faust's favorite quips, and I'd heard it from him so often by now that I didn't even bother to respond. Rather, I glanced at him. He appeared to have grown more gaunt, since our first meeting, but otherwise remained pretty much the same – the creased and dirty face, the broken teeth, the hair a rumpled disordered nest for who knows what vermin. As always, even from across the room, I caught a whiff of his body odor. Now, though, I didn't turn up my lip or wipe my runny nose. We seemed to be growing past all that.

I felt as old as Abraham, frightened and wary of the enemy, suspicious even of my mentor, Stopheles. Was that due to Faust's repeated innuendos? At least he had electricity, though it was not quite as much of a boon as I'd first thought. Our bulbs flickered and failed from time to time, sometimes cutting out completely for hours, leaving us in a long darkness. Faust usually murmured, "They'll come back on line in a few minutes," and we'd sit in the dark hoping he was right. Tonight, however, I lit a candle stub and turned to Faust. He said nothing and looked especially decrepit, hunched in his chair, his eyes closed.

"We're going to have to go out and snitch some food tonight. Midnight should give us all the cover we need and we can raid the dumpsters over by the Boulevard. Some good leavings there." It was one of the high class neighborhoods with amenities like private baths and indoor toilets, steady electricity, and decent restaurants – far beyond what most of Babylonia's population could imagine. Faust simply nodded at my suggestion without opening his eyes. Perhaps he was fitfully dozing, just semi-conscious enough to respond. I watched him for a few more moments and then noticed a slight tremor in his left hand. His arm went limp and he slipped from the chair to the floor, shaking violently. Alarmed, all I could think was *seizure!* The attack vanished almost as quickly as it had hit, but it left me more than a little shaken.

I brought the candle close, afraid Faust had suffered a stroke or even expired on the floor. Foam flecked his month and mustache, but his pupils weren't dilated. I saw his eyes consider me, saw them shift to my candle, and then he spoke, at first with difficulty, stuttering…, then more plainly and normally. "S-s-sorry to f-f-f-frighten you, f-f-f-riend." He lay there a moment and gave a weak smile: "The old Romans called it the 'falling sickness.'"

I finally exhaled and smiled just as weakly back. "Don't do that again. I'd have to lug you all the way to the Boulevard and throw you off an overpass to cover my tracks. Don't know if I've that kind of strength, let alone nerve."

"There's a spigot down at the street level," his voice raspy, his breathing ragged. "The water's pretty warm and has an odor."

Warm and *odor* sounded good enough to me. I'd drunk much worse over the last weeks. I took the steps down, two at a time, with my gallon jug, but found the pressure so low, I managed only a pint or so after five minutes. "Best I could do," I apologized when I presented it to Faust.

"It's good enough." He gulped the entire pint in one swallow and exhaled loudly. "That's better," He sighed, then saw me reach for the door again. "Leaving?"

"Food run. Wish me luck. Perhaps I'll find a fresh roast with the potatoes still warm." He nodded and I left him, to return in an hour with some moldy bread, leeks and rhubarb, and five partially open packs of beef jerky someone had thrown out. "Better than nothing," I apologized for a second time.

"Good enough," Faust quipped and launched into the meal with a zest I couldn't muster. I contented myself with another visit to the spigot and this time managed an entire container of slightly discolored liquid. Faust downed half of it.

We spent the next hour in very small, sporadic talk, during which Faust appeared progressively restored by rest and his modest meal. Whether our conversation added to his restoration was unclear, but I finally felt clear to broach the subject of his seizure. "That spell."

"What about it?" His question was toneless, but didn't warn me off.

"Unusual?"

"Not by a long shot!" To my surprise, he chuckled. "And they're not uncommon among most of us."

"Really! What's the problem? Injury? Bad food? Bad water? The last two *are* pretty plentiful in this neighborhood."

"In any neighborhood around here," Faust corrected. "It's no better on the other side of the city, not even in the rich inner suburbs where Stopheles and the other chiefs spend their weekends."

"Incredible! Why doesn't The Chief upgrade the water systems?!"

"Not incredible at all," Faust countered. "Why upgrade? Lots of us may be sick of it, but no one's dying here."

"But The Chief could make Himself more popular."

For the first time since joining me, Faust said loudly, "The Chief is quite popular. Anyway, there's no profit in upgrading the system. There's no pride in it."

"But the seizures?"

"My seizures don't come from the water and I'm not sure anyone else's does either."

"Then what causes them?"

Faust drew a long, dramatic breath: "Fear. Overwhelming, stultifying, stupefying fear. Enemy fear. Fear of everything about him. Fear of his followers." My room seemed to be growing chill, in fact downright cold, as Faust continued. A tremor traveled my spine and I stiffened, as if my own first seizure was imminent, but the feeling passed as soon as Faust paused and looked at me oddly: "You OK?"

"Yes. Yes, just having my own moment." Faust must have sensed my discomfort, my own panic-tinged disorientation.

"Don't worry," he cautioned. "You're too new here for a full blown seizure. You're not even showing symptoms yet."

"Yet."

"Relax. Really. If you were close, I'd warn you." Faust was matter-of-fact, rather than warm and comforting, but matter-of-fact was enough to calm me somewhat for the moment. "You're not betraying any of the usual symptoms."

"Symptoms? There are *symptoms?*"

"Yes, the symptoms are quite definite, very predictable." Faust sounded as if he'd stepped into some sort of professional role and was in doctor-patient mode. "You begin to feel as old as Methuselah and wary of people and their dubious promises."

O boy! I thought recognizing I had *that* symptom already.

"You shade your eyes against the evening and say nothing to strangers, hearing the shadows in their laughter. You know no one is innocent and walk a Mississippi bridge listening to suicides murmur their slurry of nightmares, water and death. You begin to fold your life away with your rags and some mornings barely choose to wear them again, hardly able to carry your burdens, weary dancer in a marathon of pain."

Perhaps it was the effect of the intense poetic quality of Faust's clinical rendition that caused me to begin to sweat profusely and I wanted him to stop. I felt like a child being told a terrifying ghost story by an older boy, the gruesome tale that made you want to squeak *Please, no! Stop! I don't want to hear any more.* But even as the sickening panic infects you, you keep your mouth shut, too much of a coward to admit you're a coward.

"Most of all you fear the enemy's people, their raw and desperate hunger. How they empty the small bowl of self, suck the sour rind of experience. Grief. Grief is their salt lick. Their eyes are not the sloe-eyed fictions of artists. They penetrate our frauds, those subtle deceits of face and what we do with our hands when no one is watching. They've heard the years of words with which we gloss the vacant center of being, breath, the tailings of mind and body. We fear their pure and generous words. Their stars deeply scar our dark."

Faust sat back looking exhausted from his short, but intense recital. I sat cold as a corpse from hearing it. "That's all I know and all you need to know. From what I can see, you're only in the earliest stages," Faust diagnosed.

"Thanks."

"You *are* welcome. Better to know what's coming, rather than be overtaken by it unawares."

"I'm not so sure about that!"

"Have it your way, but sooner or later you *will* have it."

"Enough! I'm going out!" I rose, wobbled to the door, and disappeared into the sultry night.

THE CHOSEN ONE

I dashed down our bunker's dark stairwell, like a vampire hastening back to its coffin just before dawn, and tumbled into our rooms quite winded. A sleepy Faust rolled over blinking, "Oh, it's you."

"Been gone all night."

"Find any grub?"

"Nothing, but my own stink."

Faust grunted, rolled over to face the wall, and fell into a noisy snore. I rolled onto my own cot, nervously exhausted and dead tired, but I tossed for hours before I sank into a restless sleep punctuated with vague, drifting, senseless nightmares. When I woke nearly as exhausted, full night had come round again. However, my nostrils still seemed asleep and dreaming, but not nightmares now. I sniffed: yes, I recognized aromas I never thought to smell again: the scent of yeasty fresh baked bread, pot roast and potatoes, and a mixture of vegetables – zucchini, tender asparagus spears in butter, and a side salad of lettuce, tomatoes, radishes, and broccoli, topped with ranch dressing. My stomach turned and growled so desperately, I nearly had the dry heaves on the spot. "I must be so hungry I'm making myself sick!" I cried, between choking coughs.

"The generator's failed again," came Faust's matter-of-fact comment in the dark. A match flared and I saw Faust's creased and ruined face in its momentary light, then a candle stub took flame and its soft light cast a dim dream-like glow over – yes, all the wonderful foods I'd just smelled. A bowl of ripe golden apples and pears, plums and grapes glowed in the mellow light. On Faust's table rested an apple pie and next to it a devil's food chocolate cake. I stared speechless at Faust across the repast.

"I know," he chuckled, "where did I find this!? Better I don't say and you don't know. Food thefts are worse than bank robberies and murders in The Chief's domain." His wicked smile emphasized the truth of his warning. "The only thing important at the moment is that it's here. Dig in, *but slowly now*. Our stomachs aren't used to eating so well anymore." I tried to follow Faust's suggestion and savor each mouthful. I tried chewing each fifty times before swallowing, but found myself within minutes attacking the roast with an animal ferocity, gulping half-chewed chucks of meat and potatoes. I must have looked like a food aggressive dog woofing its meal, afraid to lose it to competitors. Juice and melted butter ran down my chin and dripped on my gray tunic. I dropped as much on the floor as reached my mouth and soon splotches of mashed potatoes and wriggles of asparagus lay at my feet.

Faust for his part quietly chewed a slice of bread, a slice I recognized as the last of our old supplies. He contemplated my gobbling with more bemusement than amusement. Within twenty minutes, I felt like a gorged dog who'd nearly eaten himself to death, my stomach distended and aching. I fought to keep my rising gorge down.

Faust quipped, "And the man said, 'If I eat one more bite, I'll explode,'" and he offered me a plate with a large slice of devil's food cake, dripping with chocolate icing. "And he took one more bite…." Choking, I waved it away desperately and fell to my hands and knees, tossing the entire meal in a chaos of vomit at his feet. "….no, he didn't."

Picking myself up wearily, I raised my eyes to Faust who grimaced, "Some *bon appetite*; some thanks for all my work," and turned away while I began cleaning up my huge mess.

When I'd disposed of the stinking remains, he, apparently to show me he harbored no hard feelings over my greedy debacle, poured me a glass of something and placed two somewhat overripe grapes next to it. Thankful for something to wash the sour vomit from my mouth, I tossed down the grapes in a flash and flourished the glass in salute to him, before downing about half the glass in one gulp. In the next second, I sprayed most of it back: "Vinegar! This isn't wine. It's vinegar!"

"I didn't claim it was anything else," Faust murmured.

"You didn't say *anything*, didn't even warn me!"

"In our little world, I didn't think I should have to." He was right, of course, though that didn't make me feel any better. Even in tossing back my drink, I'd let my greed get the better of me. As I now licked the detritus of the meal from my dirty fingers, I grew suspicious. Either I'd lost my taste or the remains on my fingers lacked any. "You didn't take any food for yourself, except that stale little crust you downed while watching me."

"Why, I'd eaten long before you woke up." Faust's answer was so pat as to be outright suspicious. "A dainty little repast it was too." I eyed him like an unconvinced inquisitor, boring into him with my suspicion and he finally took umbrage at it: "What?! I try to do you a good deed and you make complete muck of it, and now you sit there as dissatisfied as ever." He was *right* there. Nothing I'd eaten had satisfied me in the least. Perhaps I was being churlish, but I wanted to sulk and half an hour passed before I was ready to speak again.

Faust, for himself, simply contemplated the darkness and left me to my irritation.

~~~~~

A boring hour later the generators snapped on and we had light again. Faust, perhaps to break the monotony, asked, "How'd you come here?"

Was he probing or was the question just a tease? "Ha! That's for me to know and you to guess!" Snap smart answers, long my stock in trade, didn't work with Faust and I should have known better than to use one.

"I sang the song of six pence, a pocket full of rye, and four and twenty black birds got baked in your pie...," Faust sang so seriously off key, my ears itched. Then, with dead seriousness, he asked again: "Do you want to tell me or shall I tell you all about it? It's either/or."

"I'd rather neither."

"Either/or – no other choice."

I was tempted to say, *Oh, the hell with it; tell away*, but decided against it for I wasn't sure I wanted to hear his version, even though he'd probably have to fall back on broadcloth generalities embroidered with guesses and falsehoods, like any mentalist or mind-reading charlatan. For an odd moment, as he awaited my answer, I felt like falling on my knees and blurting, "Forgive me, father, for I have sinned," but Faust was no father and I didn't believe in sin. The thought passed as quickly as a wave of nausea.

"It's a long story," I began.

"But shorter than you think," came his retort, almost as if he knew every word I was about to say.

"Just shut up and listen!" I spat with annoyance. "Excuse my candor, but I really have no idea how I came here."

"Sounds normal. Heard it before, lots of times"

"Sounds *normal?*"

"Forget it," Faust ordered. "I'll keep my big mouth shut. Proceed."

Fearing that Faust was playing me for the fool, I paused to see if he would cut in again, but he sat stone still and silent. I struck into that flint-like silence and sparked a conflagration in myself: "I've always seen myself as a new man for a new age. The true man of the 21st century, created in my own image, self-reliant, utterly individualistic, the post-modern American Scholar dedicated to liberty, equality, and fraternity, a dedicated deconstructionist driving my thought in a demolition derby through one belief system after another, one set of values after another, destroying them and clearing them away so the true natural human psyche might find self-realization in a b-b-brave n-new w-w-w-world." I stammered to a stop. After all, it was rather a mouthful through which I'd chewed.

"Say what?" Faust grimaced during my pause. "You speaka de English?? That mouthful of gobbledegook and polly-wolly-is-a-cracker makes no sense at all."

"Of course not. Reason is a fallacious human construct," I roared, having caught my second breath. "The Enlightenment was an unfortunate detour on humanity's road to true enlightenment. You and I know there is no such thing as truth, just your truth and my truth."

"I know no such thing," Faust muttered almost inaudibly.

I ignored his editorial distractions, was on my bow bend and not about to stem the magnificent flow of my syllables for his minor and ignorant hiccups. "Absolute truth does not exist! Absolutely does not exist! We have eaten of the Tree of Knowledge and now we know the truth, that there is no such thing as truth. We have eaten the fruit that opened our eyes to the absence of God in the scheme of things. Everything happens by chance. Everything began with nothing or perhaps another universe collided with ours and sowed the seeds of our existence. We are the measure of all things, the sum total of what we are. There is no other. There is only us and we are pre-eminent, we bright ones. Let 'the Dims' stumble about in their darkness, those sheep that drool and graze their way through life looking for a shepherd. We need none. We are Captains of our Fate, Gods in our own right. The World is ours and we have conquered it; the stars are next! We are…, we are…." I had run out of breath again, my magnificent rhetorical locomotive coasting a second time inarticulately to a halt.

Just as well. Faust had jumped on to my tracks and held up his hand, shouting, "Whoa, fella! *Whoa*! Stop before you have brain failure and I develop a terminal case of ear wax! No wonder The Chief liked you and wanted to see you. No wonder!"

"He did," I searched for words, "He did speak to my condition. He understood everything without a word from me." I felt a tad light headed just thinking back to that momentary, but magnificent meeting. Faust might not understand. I wasn't sure Stopheles would completely, but I didn't want to underestimate him. Yet The Chief had connected directly with me in the gentlest, the most unobtrusive way. He simply knew my thoughts and let me know they were His too. As I sat there opposite Faust, sat there choking on the drool of my own words, even as I remembered that meeting with The Chief, I began to grasp the feeling I'd experienced briefly when I stood before Him, the feeling I'd lately lost: that I was *special* – that I was being groomed for something far larger, far more vast than Faust could know, far beyond this paltry set of rooms. I was being tested, oriented, shown secrets few were given to see and fewer were given to understand, stepping through a training process I didn't comprehend, but had to trust, and the clown pass was part of it. Flash it in anyone's face and he stepped back and said "go on your way," because I was meant to go on my special way. Yes. I needed to get back to The Chief soon. It was as if I was one of His favorite sons and He was waiting until I reappeared and then He would embrace me fully.

"Having a spell?" Faust's voice startled me back to the present and I realized that he was leaning forward, examining my face closely and with some concern. "Brain fever? Any shakes yet? Perhaps you should lie down." Faust slipped his hand under my arm to help me up.

I slapped it aside and snarled, "Get away! I'm fine. No problem at all." Yet, again, a wave of light-headedness swept me, so I sat stark still for the next few minutes without saying anything further. But I knew! I knew now: *I was one of the chosen. No! I was THE chosen one.*

Faust shrugged his shoulders as he limped back to his seat: "OK. OK. Forget it." Later he left the bunker and I saw no more of him. *A double good riddance to you,* I thought after the first few days of his absence, *and may I never, never see you again.*

BABYLONIA PAINTED
TO LOOK LIKE ZION

This city was built (and is daily built) in imitation of Zion,
painted just like Zion. The intent of its building was to eat out Zion,
to suppress Zion, to withdraw from the truth by a false image....
-Isaac Penington

The evening of my next Stopheleon appointment arrived and I left particularly thankful that Faust was no longer about to torpedo my mood – whatever my mood was. I wasn't quite sure, but I didn't need Faust messing with my mind. That was certain. As I left, I remembered how he sometimes called out: "Watch your back!" and I'd glance around, wondering if he was referring to anything immediate. Perhaps it was his way of wishing me well, if he had it in him to wish anyone well at all.

As I began the climb toward the palaces and fortifications on the heights, I glanced back, almost expecting to see Faust in the shadows "watching my back for me" as he'd apparently done over the last months. However, the change ahead of me captured my attention as I drew closer to the main gate.

No. It wasn't another Passover disaster, no scene of collapse and dilapidation. The vast fortress and massive palaces, even The Chief's own Grand Imperium, had been transformed into something I'd seen somewhere before, some ancient, but august city replete with temples and courts and markets, square stone mansions rising one upon another. I ticked off my travels. No, the template for this was not in Italy. Not Turkey. Ephesus? Possibly, but Ephesus was larger. Alexandria? No, this city was not on a coast. In hill country? Yes, hill country! Jerusalem?

Yes. It looked like Jerusalem, exactly like Jerusalem, but far larger, far grander than ancient Jerusalem. Before me as an inflation of the original on a gargantuan scale. Here the Gate called Straight, there Solomon's great Temple with its massive walls, the pool of Siloam. Jerusalem it was! But it wasn't.... It was The Chief's palace, at least the latest remake and version of it. But at least now there was no cesspit of a moat – a definite improvement! The first guard that stopped me looked every inch an

Israelite, but the whole scene was so exact that I decided to put it to a wicked test.

"Latrine?" I put on my best strained and loaded face to emphasize I was in most urgent need. I must have succeeded in spades, because the poor fellow actually stepped back from me and pointed to a colonnade to our left. I hastened along it until I caught the whiff of urine emanating from an arched doorway to my left and I popped in. Several guards and servants stood along a stone trough relieving themselves. *Aha! Gotcha! You're uncircumcised dolts. Sorry, idiots, you've slipped up big time. You just blew the illusion!* I used the trough, humming smugly to myself and passed on my way. *OK, Stopheles. I'm ready for you. No fooling with me: I've got part of your number.*

I don't know why I felt so cocky. I'd only spotted the counterfeit and still hadn't a reason for it or a clue to what lay ahead. Whatever part of Stopheles' number I had, it still left me unable to calculate an answer to what was coming next. What's more, every time I flashed my clown coin, it only elicited a grunt and a knowing grin. A glance over my shoulder confirmed that those I'd already passed were chuckling and pointing me out to others. By the time I reached Stopheles' chamber door, my smugness had completely evaporated.

I knocked timidly. Nothing.

Harder. Still nothing!

Yet harder. I pounded and the boom of my pounding sounded hollow in the room behind the door. It didn't sound like the well appointed, fully draped, paneled and well padded chamber it had been on my last visit. I carefully turned the handle and cracked the door open. Stopheles stood with his back to me, contemplating a – a – a crucifix on the wall. A thoroughly battered, but still identifiable crucifix. I nearly fainted, knowing I shouldn't be observing the scene before me. A crucifix HERE? Right under The Chief's nose? Utterly inappropriate! Blasphemy! I opened the door another few inches and realized Stopheles was not only contemplating the thing, he *was praying, praying to it!* My duty to be The Chief's witness struggled with my urge for self-preservation, my overwhelming desire to shut the door noiselessly and vanish. Whatever I was witnessing, I knew I was completely out of my element, utterly confused. I had no way of gauging how much danger I might be in. Yet, the gossip in me got the better of me and I strained to hear. What

I heard *wasn't* a prayer. Stopheles' tone was anything but reverent, prayerful. It was bitter, cynical. Stopheles sneered from beginning to end. "They nail you back on the cross again and again and hang you in the backrooms of their lives like a curse or a warning. When did you last die for them? This morning? Last Sunday? When will you stop to realize this is no way of live – them kneeling all the years of their lives in a cheap veneration of plaster and wax? They offer you only their prayers – those small cups brimming with self –thinking they remember you. *They never do.*"

I breathed easier as I listened and saw, at the close, that he made no move to genuflect or cross himself. However that battered crucifix had come here, it was not an object of veneration. It was a tool to mock the enemy! I almost audibly exhaled with relief. I wasn't going to have to inform on Stopheles and get myself caught in the ringer of a perverse and byzantine palace intrigue.

"Come in. You're more than a little tardy." Stopheles was neither displeased with me, nor startled nor caught off guard by finding me in his doorway. Of course, with the racket I'd raised with my pounding, he'd known all along it must be me, even though he had continued to stare at the crucifix and hadn't caught physical sight of me when I first peeked in.

I stepped into the room. "I'm sorry. Everything is so different here. The place is unrecognizable. What a make-over! A JERUSALEM to dwarf Jerusalem." My admiration was unalloyed. Despite the lack of attention to, shall we say, "private" details, the change was dazzling, magnificent.

Stopheles smiled thinly. "Just one of our larger little blasphemies. The Chief calls it *His Big Mock.* I call it, *Babylonia painted to look just like Zion.*"

Then he turned and motioned toward another door, hooked his arm through mine and led out through a great expanse of garden. It was to be an intimate stroll. He had important things to tell me and he began to wax poetic:

Come. This evening we'll go for a stroll
down the world's long manicured lawns.
Look how the purple twilight gutters
in the West, how the red stars gather
over our heads and the fog's gray smoke rolls
off the stream in the valley. Here. This handsome
black cloak is just the cover you'll need to stalk
the dank coming hours. Wrap it well around
yourself and we'll walk the night like brothers
of darkness, shadows stepping like nightmares
through ten thousand thousand dreams.

Brothers of darkness! I couldn't believe my ears. All the misgivings of the past months vanished. He'd promoted me beyond my wildest hopes and desires. And so we stepped out into the frigid air, our long strides carrying us over the broken ground before us. Stopheles' spirit rose as we walked and he became effusive.

How long we've waited for a night like this!
The Chief once thought we had something going
with Moloch and his baby fed furnaces,
those Romans and their bloody games,
but to have legions of women screaming -
reproductive freedom! Hands off my body! -
though it's all about getting hands on them.

The rank and file mindlessly chanting
for the right to die! Incredible!
Who could dream it was possible
to have courts of sword-swinging-Solomons
dividing life from life, wife from husband,
mother from daughter, son from father.
Baby sacrifice, quick, legal, and safe,
backed up by the full faith and credit
of the State! Justified and sanctified
by a babble of shrewd and slippery words.

They intone them like an inexhaustible
litany of ignorance to cover every act:
We free thee, child, from poverty and abuse.
We save thee, mother, from the inconvenience.
We absolve thee, father, from all responsibility.
Grandmother, we grant thee this final gift
for thy many years: A dignified death.
Don't thank us, my dear. We'll thank you!

~~~~~

After our leisurely stroll, Stopheles and I settled into the most spacious of his elegant chambers, luxuriating in its warmth and pleasantness. Stopheles produced his best brandy and filled our glasses. Then he gave me a penetrating look and asked, "how do you like it here?"

I wasn't certain what he meant by *here*, but I was already too inebriated with myself and too exhilarated by his companionship to ask. "Fine and dandy," I laughed.

His look didn't change, but he uttered a toneless *good*. He surveyed his half empty glass and without looking up, "Where'd you take rooms?"

I was about to correct him and say *don't you mean hole-in-the-wall, or hiding place, or bunker?* but thought better of it and simply answered his query: "Over near the Boulevard."

"The Boulevard?"

"Of the Angel of Light."

"Ah, a good choice, an excellent one. How do you find it?"

Again I yearned to say, *miserable*, but once more deferred and murmured. "It's adequate." I'm afraid that sounded a tad thin, but anything more positive would be such a bald faced lie as to betray itself. However, Stopheles was not really attending to our conversation. The Boulevard had taken him elsewhere and he seemed to be talking more to himself, than speaking to me. As I listened, I caught the echoes of my prior conversation with Faust when he first introduced me to the Boulevard. It was almost as if Stopheles was speaking from the same script: how dense and crowded the city was; how The Chief was the free-thinking visionary social engineer with no qualms about the direction of

His progress; how He had displaced millions of souls and demolished a quarter of the city. And like Faust's, Stopheles' matter-of-fact tone carried no concern at all for the displaced. However, unlike in my conversation with Faust, I elected to listen meekly to Stopheles, rather than blurt something foolish. Stopheles seemed far too august, far too powerful an official, to cross.

Stopheles had shucked out of his shirt and tossed it on the floor, while he praised The Chief's dedication. He'd obviously become overheated with his liquor and the silk of his shirt was damp with sweat, the underarms soaked. He stood bare-chested, swishing his brandy about in his glass, dripping one of his over long fingers into the liquid and tasting it, smacking his lips more in the Faust manner, than in his usual delicate way. I tried to admire the room, hoping Stopheles wouldn't drop his trousers next, for clothing covers a multitude of scars and blemishes, and can make a ruined physique almost look hale and hearty. *Ruined*, indeed, was the apt word. His bare chest was pocked, marred by scores of scars, small and large. Stopheles' shoulders were boney, his arms overlong and emaciated – like his fingers, which I had always noticed and thought simply graceful and refined, until now.

"Another drink?" Stopheles was not going to allow me to ignore him in any state of dress or undress. He handed me an overfull sniffer, leered and laughed wickedly: "Drink! Drink up! The first one to the floor is the winner!" I decided to sniff and sip, rather than chug. Each glass Stopheles tossed back increased his inebriation and he was now laughing so hard that tears streamed his cheeks. Finally, to my horror, as he bent double in uncontrolled laughter over a lame joke he'd just finished telling, he lost control of his bladder, an act he didn't seem to notice - or perhaps it was beneath his dignity to notice. I forced and held a bland, non-committal smile throughout his rambling declarations and further urinations, at a loss for any better cover. He poured and downed one last brandy, wiped his tears on his sleeve and stood up, the large dark stain down the front of his silk trouser impossible to ignore. He drew a damp coin from his pocket and flipped it to me: "Here, son, you've more than earned it."

Gold! I turned it over and over in my hand. *Gold!* Stopheles, in spite of his bender, could see I was dazzled by both the size and color of this new pass. He smiled condescendingly. "Yes! Gold. Our good friend *money*. We love its subtle effects here: never enough becomes too much and our world grants its desires, its high quicksilver life. It has only to lift its hand, five fingers of indirection, its palm an empty salute. It grows to love the dark impertinence of men, to cultivate the grave indifference that shadows truth."

At the close of his short rendition, Stopheles scratched his chest, rubbed his damp groin, and ordered, "Now off with you! I must change for a meeting with Our Chief." Dismissed! Finally! An abrupt dismissal I received with immense relief. We drank a quick, shallow, informal toast to The Chief and I departed, clutching my coin. It had been a long, exhausting night and I still had a long, rough trek back to the bunker, but, despite Stopheles' disturbing behavior, I was too elated to care. I'd been tested and not found wanting. I'd gone in with the bronze and brought home the gold. I'd been elevated to the Brotherhood and walked now with the mighty. Satisfied for once, I had one of the best sleeps of what was finally becoming a more satisfactory existence.

SATISFACTION IS AT BEST
A FICKLE MISTRESS

I can't get no satisfaction,
I can't get no satisfaction,
'Cause I try and I try and I try and I try,
I can't get no, I can't get no
-M. Jagger & K. Richards

Satisfaction has always struck me as a fickle mistress, given to serial betrayals, so I was not surprised, merely crestfallen, when I awoke back in the bunker hours later, awoke more dissatisfied than I had been since I arrived in Babylonia. As I surveyed my dank and gloomy room, its cracked and stained walls and spotted, frayed carpet, the reality of my situation began to weigh upon me.

My existence seemed, not more satisfactory, but less. Whatever possessed Stopheles to drop so out of character, as he did last night? Was it a momentary lapse, like we all have? *Too, too out of character.* Had a mask dropped revealing his truer nature? And for me to rave about promotion and elation like I did?! Promotion? *To what?* Elation? *About what?* About Stopheles' cynical descriptions of the nature of money and the decadent characters of men and women? I was elated from drinking with one of the big dogs and watching him pee his pants? Perhaps there was something in the Brandy. Neither its aroma nor its taste seemed quite right. The only things I'd brought home were a grubby self, a hangover, and my gold coin.

My gold coin! I checked the trousers I'd worn. Not there. Fumbled for it on my night table, but only succeeded in knocking over the stub of an unlit candle and a half finished can of beer. After an hour of frantic searching, I found the coin by my door. I examined it up close, scratched it with a stone. Gold?? Not gold. Gold plated? ("No, you brainless dolt!" Faust would shout at me later. "Not gold, stupid. Not even gold plated. Low grade fool's gold. Isn't worth the energy used to smelt it or the die used to imprint it").

Fool's gold. Why wasn't I scandalized? I wasn't even surprised. The image on the face of the coin was worn to faintness, as if it had been fingered, rubbed, shined, and studied by a host of former owners. *Who were they? And where were they now?* I quickly thrust those two questions to the back of my mind, feeling that to examine them too rigorously might lead me up against some very unsound and undesirable conclusions.

Later, under the electric lights and with a magnifying glass, I'd managed to trace the facial image and the faint "inscription" on the rear. The coin's face appeared to be imprinted with the head of a monarch or emperor. Engraved on the rear were the words, *Forever Defiant* in Latin, two clear numbers – 66 -, and the vague outline of a rampant jackal. The placement of the numbers slightly off center suggested that there might have been a third digit, but it had been worn away.

On occasion, when sleep absolutely refused to come, I pulled my new jackal pass from my pocket and examined it: a counterfeit denarius, perhaps? A denarius with the head of an old Roman Emperor on it. But who? Augustus? Tiberias? Marcus Aurelius? Not Nero, no. Julian, maybe? Julian the Apostate? I'd always enjoyed reading Roman history and particularly the lives of the Imperial emperors, their incredible excesses and perversions. The problem was there were so many emperors, especially as the empire decayed and the Romans often insisted on running through a half dozen or so in less than that number of years. Finally, after a night's hard thought, the identity of the likeness punched into my consciousness. *Caligula!*

Thereafter my meditations on the coin took unexpected, startling turns. Why Caligula? Chief among the most perverse emperors. An adulterous, incestuous monster who murdered his own impregnated sister by cutting the fetus out of her womb. A sadistic ruler who suborned the whole government with his maniacal desires and who delighted in ordering Senators who claimed they were willing to die for him to carry out that deed immediately as a sign of their utter loyalty. Had Stopheles used the coin simply because it was readily at hand? Or was it an item in his collection he was particularly proud of – or perhaps one that carried special and ominous meaning? A message? For me?

Perhaps Stopheles had no idea whose image was on the coin, but I couldn't quite give credence to that hope. He was simply too well read and perverse enough, I knew now, to be drawn to a nature like Caligula's.

No. I could no way justify the argument that I'd been given the coin by chance. As I considered everything that had transpired since my first night in The Chief's kingdom, I couldn't believe anything here happened quite by chance, unless it was by a perverse chance. The more I studied the coin, the more misgivings swam into my mind. Did Caligula prefigure terrible perverseness ahead? Or lavish excess? Or mindless cruelty? Appalling violence? Whatever I thought I'd received from Stopheles, I now knew I held a worthless and well worn pass and felt little, if any, desire to utilize it, no desire to visit the version of Stopheles I'd witnessed. One thing I grasped as I held the pass in my palm. I couldn't pass the coin on to someone else. I couldn't toss it in the rubbish somewhere in the city. No. Not that I couldn't. I *dare* not. Yes, I *dare not*. Whatever I was destined to face at the next meeting, I wouldn't be allowed to avoid it. Stay locked in my room and someone or something would come for me. Disappear into the bowels of the city outside and "they" would purge the place to flush me out. There was really only one way to rid myself of the thing: *return-to-sender*. Utilize it for the purpose it was intended. I'd have to trek back to The Chief's palace and present my pass once more, hoping against hope that my nightmares were simply wild figments of what had become my paranoid and fevered imagination. Despite the musty humidity of the bunker, I felt chill and shuddered, staggered toward my sofa, weeping uncontrollably.

Was I losing it?! I must be! My mind running amok; my bowels churning with anxiety, a berserker in chaos – *that's* what I was acting like! I collapsed on the sofa and slid off onto the floor, my heart beating triple time. "Deep breaths, deep breaths, deep breathes," I repeated over and over, until slowly my panic passed. The generators failed and kicked back on, failed and kicked in again over the next hours, but I hardly noticed, my inner darkness more cloying than any outward darkness could be. Finally I felt able to stand again, having clawed my way back into fragile possession of myself.

Throughout the ensuing hours, the thought grew in me that only a visit to The Chief could heal and restore me. Only He could re-infuse me with my lost confidence. Given my fragile state, I kept myself closeted in the bunker. It wasn't difficult. The place was a secret fortress and in the neighborhood in which it was hidden – if I could call it a neighborhood – no one looked out for anyone else. When I walked the narrow, filthy, broken streets, the area appeared to be the model for a 20th century communist "workers' paradise" – grim, somber, gray, a place where the inhabitants went about their business with their heads down. Eye contact was grounds for suspicion, an open gathering of friends might be construed as conspiratorial. It was safer to keep to oneself, to keep off the streets, and to hurry back to one's bolt hole, after one retrieved some food and supplies.

As a precaution, I slept in an alley twice or thrice, instead of returning to my room, then the next day checked thoroughly for signs of disturbance there, but couldn't find the least little hair out of place, not even the one I'd place across the door jam to alert me that someone had entered. Nor did my so-called neighbors betray any awareness that I'd been gone or that something was afoot concerning me. Believe me, I watch my neighbors closely, straining to spy some change in demeanor that would speak to my comings and goings having been noticed or, worse, that someone had been making inquiries about me. After a month of lurking and shirking, drifting through the slums like an unacknowledged ghost, after a month of starting at every voice that sounded a bit louder than usual, I was pretty well broken down.

~~~~~

So as this evening passed from penumbra to umbra, I tossed and sweated on my cot, searching in vain for sleep. I lay awake for hours, listening into the stale silence, hearing absolutely nothing until -

A scratch!

An utterly inconsequential rasp, like a fingernail against wood. At my door! It took me a moment to collect my wits and compose myself. I listened intently for a minute or two and –

There it was again, this time two quick rasps.

I tiptoed over and put my ear to the bunker door. Was a mouse or rat pawing? Lots of both around here – and their fleas too. No. The third time I heard, not the light scratching, but two taps. Two taps - a pause – then three more. Light, hardly audible, but still definite. Someone was trying to catch my attention without catching the attention of anyone else. "Who's there?" I whispered in my best stage whisper, immediately feeling as foolish as those idiots in horror films who call out those same words, as the lurking menace closes on them.

"Me," came the stage whispered reply.

"Who's me?"

"Faust! Open the stupid door!" He sounded both anxious and desperate. Even with my hand on the latch, I hesitated. Why now? Why here? The man who I'd often suspected would betray me and whom I had in turn tried to betray. The so-called companion who claimed he watched my back and then simply disappeared. But he didn't sound angry or wrathful. His voice lacked even a hint of his usual deviousness. I still hesitated, remembering Judas and his posse, wondering if Faust had brought back-up.

"*Please!*" It was a plea, not a demand, slightly louder than before.

I – I – I opened the door and he tumbled into the room.

He rose to his feet with some difficulty and dusted himself off. "Thank you," he whispered. His "thank you" was not really a grateful one, more ironic and tinged with irritation. "Looks like I finally lost 'em."

"Lost *who*?"

"Whoever or whatever was following me," he still whispered

"And you led them HERE!"

"Not here. I lost them blocks back, up by the Boulevard. They lost my scent. I made sure they were running in circles without a clue to the direction I'd gone. This little bolt hole is too valuable to risk."

I simply stared at him. Our lighting had begun to flicker making my face appear a mask of disbelief and unalloyed suspicion, and after a moment he must have realized how unwelcomed his reappearance was. To my surprise, he whispered an utterly sincere, "I'm sorry," but it only annoyed me and I was tempted to retort, "We don't accept apologies here." I'd learned that no one was really sorry here, except may be sorry for themselves. No more being easily taken in! Not me! Faust always trumped his apologies with too many rude put-downs, too many unapologetic betrayals.

"Yeah, right! About what?" I spat back, making clear I was not in a mood to accept easy apologies.

"About my behavior – warm and cold. About my 'chip-on-my-shoulder' attitude."

I continued to stare at him, silent and cool. I wasn't about to turn my back on him.

"Sorry for calling you a 'dumb, arrogant stupid bastard.' Sorry for my lack of trust and trustworthiness."

"So…?"

"Sorry you concluded I was out to betray you."

"Well, you *were*, weren't you?"

"Absolutely not, *but you were*. You were ready to betray me." That drove the nail of truth into my heart, and finally I turned away.

"Yes. I was. I admit it. But how do I know you weren't out of get me."

Faust smiled for the first time: "Well, you've not been gotten, have you?"

"No. Not at least *yet*," I added to emphasize I still had lingering suspicions. However, I was beginning to relax, willing to hear him out. "It would have been difficult to get me, though. I've been laying extremely low."

"You call what you've been doing 'extremely low'?" He looked at me as if I was more than slightly mad.

"Yes. How do you know *what* I've been doing to stay out of sight?"

"Because you've been in sight most of the time," Faust said with a soft matter-of-factness that convinced me he considered it the truth. Then he added his final card: "I've been watching your back."

"Watching my back?!" I was flabbergasted at his claim. "Not that old canard again. Don't even try it!"

"On the contrary, I've seen almost your every move, including your tipping a few with your bare-chested lover Stopheles."

I was speechless. I simply stared at Faust, but the longer I stared, the more it dawned on me that what he claimed was true. He finally broke the silence.

"By the way, how is Stopheles these days?"

"You tell me!"

"I can't," he confessed. "You don't think I have walk-in privileges. In fact, most days, I'm all but on the run and can't go near that place." I was crowded with questions. I wanted to assault him with a mean, thoroughgoing, painful interrogation, but realized I'd have time for that later. I chose instead of answer Faust's question.

"Stopheles? Not the fellow I thought he was; not anything I can pin down."

"You're making progress."

"Progress in what?"

"Just progress."

Instead of answering my question, Faust drove on: "Sounds like they're using the same old process as usual. Of course, it almost always works, so I can't blame them."

"Process? Works?"

Now it was Faust's turn to look incredulously at me. He shook his head: "Nearly at the end of the whole process and not a clue."

I recovered more quickly than before: "Not a clue, maybe, but lots of suspicions."

"Lots of suspicions," he rejoined, "lots of confusion."

I nodded: "Yes. *Lots* of confusion.

"No surprise there! Paranoia is a wonderful disease. It feeds on everything it sees!"

WHAT ADAM AND EVE CAME TO KNOW

This is that first story
which men and women tell
over with literal tongue,
not feeling that old serpent
side-wind a mouthful:
a fig of a story,
how we cover ourselves
when we see one another,
broken twigs of promise
scattered between us,
and Eden is only
a place where we hide
in fear from the truth.

When confused, hide! After my last meeting with Stopheles I was confused and shaken enough to deem hiding a basic necessity – something made possible by the presence of Faust. For the next few weeks, he was my sole contact with the outside world, bringing in needed food, supplies, and occasional rumors as he came across them. I actually grew modestly thankful for his presence as I settled into a bunker routine and tried to sort out where I stood in the grand scheme of Babylonia

A rumor circulated that I'd vanished, like so many before me. My disappearance really didn't cause even the most miniscule ripple in the dark waters here, no, not even the slight shimmer a water spider makes as it skates on the surface tension of a pond. The Chief's subjects don't talk openly about vanishings and disappearances. Ask "Where's Stew?" or "What happened to Tony?" or "Haven't see Melissa around – bogeyman get her?" and the shrug is enough to tell you "Don't ask again." Ask "Can you tell me where I can find him?" and it will elicit only a general inspection of shoes or sandals, clogs or clodhoppers. A deep tone of concern in your voice, even to a seemingly braver soul than most, will return at best a murmured, "Mum's the word, mate." I once heard one of The Chief's under-chiefs bark, "Sent elsewhere! That's all you'll know and all you need to know." No one ever learns anything more, but our dark imaginations fill in a rather large blank canvas with lurid nightmares, all the dire possibilities. No garden of earthly delights, I can promise you.

Anyway I had been out of circulation for some weeks, hiding from the proverbial knock on the door or avoiding that Some-Such that does more than go bump in the night. Faust proved more of a reliable Bro' than I would ever have expected, because no one appeared to arrest me. No betrayer him!

Or then again, perhaps he was waiting, storing up a kindling of lies and betrayals toward some future conflagration. Or perhaps he just didn't give a rat's whisker what happened to me. The last seemed more and more likely: he just didn't care. When I did step out from hiding, a little less certain of myself, a little more moth-and-worm eaten but still vaguely recognizable, no one seemed surprised to see me. Some just flashed a gap-toothed grin. Others pointed and tittered and let me know I was the butt of some rather unpleasant and derogatory gossip. This latter was more disconcerting to me. I'd become something of a joke in my absence and I'd no idea why.

However, as I began to circulate outside the bunker again, I found Faust's supportive role decayed rapidly. His somewhat helpful and occasionally apologetic demeanor proved to be two more false facades, discarded as soon as they no longer served his purposes. Then, quick as the first buzz from a rattlesnake's tail, he returned to the old Faust: quizzical, circumspect, secretive, non-committal, unconcerned most clearly about me. Yes, he was his usual self: blunt, rude, insulting, argumentative, annoying to the *n-th* power. He could be maddeningly indefinite about almost everything. Didn't even inquire about my comings and goings. So I got blunt: "Don't you care?"

"Whatever for?!"

"Perhaps I'll lose my way, slip and fall into the some pit, down to some dire level beyond help?"

"Where do you think you are now?" Faust surveyed me as if I were a complete fool, but only quipped, "A pit? Some dire level? Rather Dantesque, aren't you?"

"And what's wrong with being Dantesque?" I shot back. "You yourself said 'he knew who and what he was dealing with.'"

"Yeah! '*Who* and *What*,' but not *Where*. Oh, he was through here all right, but...".

"But he even drew a map!" I exclaimed.

"Some map! What a tame and orderly imagination the poor soul had. The man was all pits and levels, vents and brimstone lakes, sulfurous archipelagoes and frozen tundra. Whether stepping down or stepping up, whether in the Inferno or Purgatory or even Paradise, always the levels! The man did love his levels. You seen any of that stuff around here?"

"No. But I haven't seen much of 'here' either."

"Well taken. True." I couldn't believe my ears. A compliment from Faust! "But you've got time on your hands, eons of it. The Boulevard always beckons us over the next rise and over the next rise we find the Boulevard that always beckons us over the next rise and over the next rise we find the Boulevard that always...."

"All right already!" I kicked a chair, fisted an overstuffed sofa, raising a cloud of dust from the latter. We were back to our old annoying repartee. I braced myself for some ripe obscenity or even a flash of violence, but Faust seemed to ignore my disrespect and just shook my dust off his feet.

"Just don't expect levels. Nobody graduates from here, either up or down," Faust muttered, his tone rather glum now.

"No levels. But that's not logical." I knew he'd set me up, as soon as the words left my tongue.

"*Of course not!*" It was a retort with the force of a roundhouse punch. "Where do you think you *are?!* Nothing's logical around here. Haven't you begun to figure that out? This place is the original deconstructionist's dream!" He was dressing me down and mocking me all at the same time. "This is chaos. *Chaos!*"

I decided I wouldn't be intimated by his browbeating. "Well, Chaos Theory *does* have a logic of its own!" I admit it was a lame return and he fired it right back across the net into my face.

"Damn your theory. And damn your logic. This is *CHA-OS! REAL CHA-OS.*" I nearly fainted from his hot, fetid breath in my face. "Don't give me no silly human rationality. You should be beyond that here and now." Without a word left to call my own, I sat down heavily, winded by the whole exchange.

And Faust? He strutted up and down before me, chin up, hands behind his back, like a victorious Napoleon. Sometimes I think that I think best on my behind, for as the moments wore on and I contemplated the tiny creepy-crawlers in the dirt on our tattered carpet, a whole different question formed itself up.

In my mind, I was back in the beginning, ticking over the whole Adam and Eve thing, and when the serpent lisped - "your eyes will be opened, and you will be like God, knowing good and evil"[4] - I had it. I had my question and shot to my feet so quickly, I startled Faust for once. "*What* did they come to know?" I asked with a levelness that emphasized the very seriousness of my question.

"What did *who* come to know? And about *what?*" He was annoyed by my initial lack of clarity, but I didn't care. I was pursuing serious business now.

"Adam and Eve, that's *who*. And what did they come to know when they became 'like God, knowing good and evil'?"

To my surprise, Faust laughed. "So you finally teased that out of your lame little mind, huh? You know, it ain't the key to it all, to all the secrets, to everything."

"Don't try to put me off. I asked a legitimate question."

"Yes, but only about an illegitimate statement," he was verbally fencing with me, but he'd left himself open for once and I lunged.

"You're saying The Chief makes illegitimate statements?" I felt I'd pinned him, but he parried me quite unexpectedly.

"Of course."

"And does He know you think so?"

"Of course."

"Perhaps that's why The Chief distrusts you." We were both working ourselves up into a smug sweat.

"Of course not. He knows what I think, because I know who I'm dealing with.'

"And I don't?" Now it was his turn to thrust and he nicked me good.

"Not on your wretched life."

I turned desperate. I charged: "You're calling The Chief a common liar then?"

He laughed uproariously, laughed until his tears mixed with dirt in the creases of his face and flowed like cheap mascara. I stood there, quite deflated, yes, defeated too. "The Chief? A common liar? *Au contraire*, silly fellow: Nothing common about Him! Call Him the pinnacle of lying's aristocracy: the exceptional, effusive king of lies! He's so damned good He even lies with truth.

"Take Eve, that stupid little woman. He gave her two dogs and a ruby, two lies and a truth, and don't you dare claim she was innocent or ignorant. She *knew* the truth and the truth was *Don't eat that stinking, rotten, wormy apple!*

"She could've said, *Oh no! You lying rascal. I know the truth and you won't be turning me into no goddess. Quick slither your way back to hell before I stomp your head!* That woulda rattled Him real bad and He'd have low tailed it outta there, but she didn't say that, did she? She listened when He lisped, 'you'll be like God, knowing good and evil,' and He precisely struck 'like' and don't give me that cheap politician's *depends on how you define 'like.' Like* is like, fool. Understand English? Like *God* isn't *being God*. Huge thunder and lightning difference I'd say!

"She knew the truth and chose to bite and it was no dainty little chew either, but a quick and greedy mouthful, juice running down her chin, big ugly grin on her face. No, she shouldn't have, but, O! It tasted so, so very good!

"Truth among the lies! Truth among the lies, wording precise and fine as a razor cut to draw the almost imperceptible line between good and evil. Sounds good to you? Sounds good to me! Let's bite and be done with it, done as damnation."

I must confess his rhetoric dazzled me and he ended it with a light-footed jig before me, as if daring me to *match that!* I let him know it was worth only a half dozen claps of mock applause on my fake applause-meter. I made my feeble point, but paid for it, my chapped hands stinging from even those few slaps.

Faust was still beyond me. He simply grinned and considered his broken fingernails like a woman fresh from a bad nail salon. I should have quietly walked away at that point, but instead I clutched the last straws of my ego and demanded the answer to my question: "So what if The Chief lies on occasion. He's brilliant. I'm sure He has His reasons and that they're good ones. So what?"

"Indubitably, my dear Watson. *So what.*"

"But *you*, my dear Fassie," (that cut him – I could see it), you're not so brilliant (cut number two – I planted my feet squarely and glowered at him). *You* didn't answer my question! So Adam and Eve became like gods and knew good and evil. Vague, sir! Abstract, sir! What did they come to know *really?*"

I felt for a second as if he was deciding whether he should just murder me and be done with it or tender me the answer I demanded. I fully expected the former. His hands twitched as with a palsy and he swallowed thrice before he could find voice. Then he spoke with remarkably even control: "What did they come to know? Just what it said: good *and evil.*

"*Don't play me,*" I said it with all my own suppressed rage, but he didn't even blink. He rose, walked calmly to his room, and I heard him rummaging about there, muttering, "Now where is that stupid pack of....HA!" Faust returned with a dog-eared, tattered volume, scarlet of cover, though the title had worn off. He placed it in my hands.

"I'm not playing you. Did Stopheles give you your very own copy of The Chief's *Salms?* He must be slipping!"

"The Chief wrote *Psalms?!*"

"Not *Psalms,* dumb, dumb, S-A-L-M-S: *Salms!*"

"*Salms.* Yeah."

"Yeah, he give 'em to you??"

"No, he didn't."

"All, for...," I fully expected a head-slap for my obtuseness, but Faust simply opened the book to a greasy, smudged page, pointed me to the text and said, "Best description I ever saw of what Adam and Eve came to know."

SALM 13

After that first bite, they proceeded to chew
their way over the whole tree, nibbled each
golden and scarlet globe like small green worms.

They even sucked at the core's bitter seeds
and the tree shrank into itself as did
the ruined landscape around them.
They slept a restless nightmare sleep

and woke to bathe in the cold Euphrates,
but found nothing came clean, neither the earth
soiled with their droppings nor the air fouled
by their cackle and hack. Whatever they

thought was promised, they knew only the
skull's a shell easily shattered, the heart
a fist of bloody gristle. And the bowels?
The bowels are hardly the seat of affection.

After I'd read the *Salm,* not once, but thrice, I looked up at Faust. He stared back at me a long while, but I refused to drop my eyes. Finally, he whispered: "That's what they came to know. Satisfied?"

"No."

"Neither were they."

HELL'S OLD GUERILLA WAR

In spite of our bouts of combativeness, Faust and I often now found ourselves talking in whispers late into the night, letting the dark add its insulating cloak to what I deemed were our forbidden conversations. In the weeks that followed, we began to compare notes and experiences, explored the oddities of the 'pass' system, Stopheles' shape shifting character, even some other palace minions, whose strange proclivities and grotesque appearances made me feel fortunate not to have met them. As we wound down into weariness each night, one unanswered question continued to tease my mind.

"One last question," We'd talked so much, even my whisper was strained and hoarse. "Why did you decide it was time to reappear again?"

"Because it was time. We're about to have another invasion of the body snatchers." Faust thrust his finger in my face like a recruiting poster mockery and growled, '*The Chief Needs YOU!*' The Chief's press gangs are back again right on schedule and, while I know how to avoid 'em, if you keep creeping around, you'll be swept up this time, pass or no pass.

"Press gangs again? Aren't they ever satisfied? *For what?!* Is He, are we, at war?" As soon as I asked, I felt like the simplest of simpletons.

"The Chief's always at war. He's been at war since the beginning of time and He'll keep it up until the very end of days. He calls it His *old guerilla war* and that's a pretty good description of it. It's a bloody business, something to dodge at all costs if you can. There's no glory in the fight, no victory, only a never-ending agony out on the universe's burned over battle fields.

"No victory? Why fight at all then?

"Ah, there you have the crux of the matter: As The Chief says, His 'purpose holds to wreck the enemy's world with scalding chaos, to eviscerate and skin the enemy's image in every soul we capture.'"

Faust could see I was far from convinced that such a war without victory was worth the effort and the agony, so he enlarged and clarified The Chief's motivation. "He loves it. He loves the war, the gargantuan struggle, the ancient and on-going refusal to surrender. It literally invigorates – no – it supercharges Him!"

I still had trouble getting my mind around that motivation, so Faust added, "If the gangs impress you, you'll be in for the mother of all wars, for

> "The Chief loves it when the blood runs fast,
> when hatred floods the land with scarlet death.

My advice is: keep that empty head of yours down and your fat derrière well camouflaged from both The Chief and His enemy.

> "You'll understand why if one of the Enemy's
> quick patrols armed with Eden's flaming lances
> catches you in the open. Each stroke will
> scorch and sear your flesh. You'll stagger back,
> briefly blinded and breathless, for an instant
> only a faded negative of yourself."

Faust considered the effect of his words, then convinced he'd not emphasized the danger enough, asked. "Haven't read *The Satanic Sorrows* all the way through, have you?"

I colored. I'd riffed the pages of Stopheles' gift, read three or five of the items, then ignored the rest.

"Never much of a reader, were you?" Faust asked.

"Nope."

"Some be, even here! Let me recite something from that little book:

> "The enemy's *never* surprised by us,
> by our ferocity, *never* tricked and fooled.
> You'll see our horses prance and rear, ready
> to bolt, and our horsemen – starved and gaunt –
> shift and cough and try to catch their breath.
> It's impossible to overestimate the enemy's
> strength. To think you can trifle with him
> is instant suicide. To drum assembly here
> for battle is to call all his massive legions
> down on us, each sword and spear
> a searing exclamation point of light.

Move and our enemy moves; stand firm
and he appears everywhere around us.

"The Chief knows our only chance is stealth
against such swiftness. Ambush an archangel
here, a troop of angels there. Try to rake
black suppurating evil across their brightness,
then disappear like hungry ghosts."

"You make it sound like a sorry rear guard action, like we're defeated, even as we fight. That's crazy. That makes no sense. Why even fight?!"

"Crazy or not," Faust explained with unusual patience, "once each war or battle has begun, there's no going back. More armies than you realize went to battle knowing they were already defeated. Yamamoto knew it, even as he launched his planes on Pearl Harbor. Hannibal and his men fought in Italy for a dozen years after realizing Carthage had decided to write them off. And all Lincoln's early generals who found Robert E. Lee had already secured the best ground on the battlefield: they still sent their regiments and divisions into the meat grinder, all the while knowing the battle was lost."

"And the men? What did they think?"

Faust shrugged as the bunker's lights winked out, then came up again. "The men weren't asked. They're not expected to think. They're ordered to fight, and fight they did, often heroically. You asked, 'why even fight?' Because once you're in that army of the damned, *you must.* Fight and the enemy will likely destroy you. Run away and your own will execute you as a traitor and a coward. Keep your empty head down and your derrière covered and perhaps you'll survive to fight and die another day."

"That stinks!"

"Yep! It stinks as high as all those corpses piled on the battlefield."

SISTER FAUSTINA WAS RIGHT

*"There is nothing so banal and stupid as an intellectual
trying to make sense of hell, or worse, denying its existence."*

In spite of our hours of jibes and counter-jibes, our insults and put-downs, Faust was growing on me. Don't get me wrong. He'd grown on me like a tolerable parasite that sucks down my energy levels, but leaves me alive. He'd never, never, never be a bosom-buddy. We annoyed one another days on end; made war, not love; hurled sharp exchanges and fired salvos and broadsides of insults back and forth until one of us was annoyed and insulted enough to shut down or shut up. Yet, I found even within our bitterest brawls an odd bond appeared to be forming, one that finally allowed me to risk a question that had nagged at me for months. There was no way to preface the question, to soften it, to make it easy to swallow and respond to, so I simply blurted it at the end of one of our grubs: "You said The Chief likes you, but doesn't trust you. How come?"

To my surprise, Faust wasn't surprised or annoyed at the query. He simply grunted and swallowed: "How come He likes me? Or how come He doesn't trust me?"

"Both."

"That's a very long story!"

"Well, wouldn't you say you've got more than all the time in the world to tell it?" I had Faust there. Indeed, we had all the time to the end of days.

"Aye, you're right!" He decided not to play our usual little game of questions and excuses, a game that almost always deflected us away from any matter at hand. He rather considered where to begin. That, in itself, was more than unusual and I suspected a ruse somewhere ahead. He mumbled and murmured through several false starts: *Let me explain it this – no. Perhaps it's best to – hmmm – perhaps not. Well now, we can. No we can't....* Finally he found a thread of the story he could tug on and pull out. "I was born to enemy parents in Roda in Weimar. Even in my early years, my father deemed me to be lacking in common sense and my mother was equally convinced I lacked wisdom, so they concluded I was fit only to be a scholar." Faust cast me a wicked sideways glance at that, one which I made an intensely studied effort to ignore.

"And what exactly did you study?"

"I started with medicine but illness and suffering bored me – or maybe they overexcited me. Whatever. I was impatient with my patients and sometimes cursed them, because they took so long to die. I liked the play of Mathematics more. Numbers held a certain fascination for me, but I found I'd soon mastered all there was. At that time, there was little Calculus, no advanced Mathematical theory. Math soon proved pretty mundane and easily exhausted by a student like me. No, I put Medicine and Mathematics out for the bone and rag collector, seeking something deeper, more powerful, more challenging, something that could divert me for all my years, and then some. Something that could give me everything I desired: riches beyond compare, power greater than that of kings and queens, the fulfillment of every earthly desire. I wanted it all and I needed to find the way to get it."

"Ambitious weren't we?" I jibed, but Faust ignored me now in return, too interested in recounting his own story.

"I studied Astrology next and that led me to Sorcery and from Sorcery, I found it only a small step to master Necromancy, and then I knew what I must do to grasp all my ends and bind them together." He paused for such a long time, that I thought he'd abruptly finished his tale, or more likely fallen asleep in the gloom. Then Faust's voice rose, thin and strained, "I would use The Chief. I would summon Him against His will and make Him submit to me."

His confession, if I can call it that, so staggered me, I barely exhaled my retort. "But He submits to no one, certainly not to such as us, let alone the enemy. *Ever!*"

Faust didn't contradict me. He simply shrugged his shoulders, as if my observation had nothing to do with his story. "Oh, I summoned Him all right. One night in Spesser Wood outside Wittenberg. First, I raised a great storm to cover my work and then laid my Pentagrams and circles, worked my most powerful charms and incantations, and with forked flashes of lightning and drum rolls of thunder, The Chief appeared, more than a little irritable at having been turned from his usual pursuits."

"Pursuits?"

Faust waved my query aside. "'Hoar frost and Hell Hounds, what are you doing, boy!?' Our Chief roared."

Faust smirked: "I smiled to myself – perfect proof I possessed the power over Him I'd sought – and I roared back: 'I have called thee for the simple purpose of negotiation. We will sort out an agreement to my liking.'"

"'I will, will I?!' He growled and spat a shower of sparks, "Not on your life!" And He darkened the night yet further with a great angry sweep of his black wings.

"Oh," I smiled. "there you are wrong: it will be *on my life*." I said it with such confidence, yea, smugness that The Chief must have perceived something of Himself in me – and He appeared to reconsider His position.

He circled me, looking me up and down from every angle, but found that I stood rooted and unmoving, utterly sure He could do nothing ill to me. After several moments of heavy breathing, during which He appeared to be struggling to control Himself, He began to relax and appeared willing at least to discuss and listen. With the circumspect caution of a master negotiator, He belched, "And what might I be expected to agree to?"

I instantly spread my hand before Him. "First, *you* will serve me so long as *I* live. Second, *you* will provide *me* with all the knowledge, wealth, and power I ask. And third, you will never lie to me." At this third demand, He stranged for a moment, His vast wings sweeping the dank air into a mini-maelstrom of thunder claps. Then He stilled and seemed to embrace my third demand with a gentle laugh.

"*Never lie to you*. Now why should I have to lie to such as you?"

I wasn't about to let The Chief begin to pretzel my points: "*Those* are my *nonnegotiable* demands."

The Chief frowned darkly, but drew a long hot breath and spoke quietly in measured sentences. "You forced me here to this dank and dripping forest to negotiate an agreement. That *suggests* to me that I may either make a counter offer or at least detail some simple expectations on my side for granting such power and being bound under your direction and for your purposes." He spoke with such controlled dignity that I momentarily swelled with a rush of megalomania...

…but grew wary in the next instant. Just what counter offers might he make in an attempt to shave my power away and gain the upper hand? *Watch yourself, I muttered to myself: Here it comes.* "What might be your counter offer?"

The Chief stunned me, when He confessed, "I have none to make. I don't have the power to refuse such demands, *do I?*"

I swooped down on that: "No. You *don't.*"

"Then," He, who is never humble, began almost humbly, "I ask only three things."

"And what might they be?" I spoke like an Overlord dictating terms to a defeated enemy, and I was in no mood to trifle.

"First, you renounce your Christian faith."

"Done!" He had my instant agreement. After all, I'd never taken it seriously nor practiced even its simplest rituals and prayers. Christians were weak demented simpletons. What a cheap and easy demand of no consequence!

"Second, I gain your body and your soul at the close of 30 years of serving you." The Chief spoke as if He was reciting in monotone the broiler plate of His standard contract. I smiled inwardly at this, for being the more powerful of the two in these negotiations, I'd be able to renegotiate any time I wanted to and alter our agreement even more to my benefit.

"No problem!" I assented and drew a long breath, steeling myself inwardly to resist Him and force Him back in line, if He tried any of His usual tricks to negate what we'd already agreed to.

"The last is simple: that you sign our pact with your signature in your own blood. You need not worry; such things only take a few drops."

"Standard operating procedure, huh?"

"Of course," His voice, which is truly never meek, sounded almost meek – and He bowed to emphasize our agreement.

I breathed with easy relief: "Fair indeed and for my side, I do agree." The Chief, too, seemed relieved and squared his huge shoulders, folding his great wings behind his back. His broad and easy smile gave me a moment's pause, but we readily drew up the formal document and signed it.

I eyed Faust for several moments. My next question was the big one and I wondered, first, if he was ready to answer it, and, if he was, what that answer would prove to be. After all, The Chief was a master negotiator and I'd never met anyone here yet who claimed to have bested Him. "So, did The Chief keep His part of the bargain?"

To my surprise, Faust announced, "To the final letter!"

"He served you."

"Most excellently!"

"And He provided everything you wished, knowledge…."

"I became the foremost scholar in Europe, did I not?"

"Indeed you did," I had to agree that even in the 21st century, his fame was undiminished.

"And He never lied to you?"

The Chief's keeping that demand seemed incredible, but Faust's testimony was convincing. "He never had to. After all, He had the pact."

"He had the pact," I repeated Faust's words over to myself, but their significance took some time to dawn on me.

Faust tried to explain: "The Chief had the pact. I had my thirty years of unfettered access to Him. He had me signed and sealed, deliverable at the end of thirty years. He had no need of lying and trickery."

I thought a long time, searching the problem from a multitude of angles, but could find no value in The Chief having the pact. I protested, "You, yourself, planned to escape, to trick The Chief at the last moment. Your signature was a red lettered lie."

"Exactly," Faust assented. "I had several escape routes mapped out, so that if one failed, I'd have others. I wanted to hear The Chief intoning His old Welsh lament, but intoning it about *me*, you know, the one He sang when the crusty ol' Welshman duped him."

"Old Welsh lament?" I continued to look blank. Someone else had beaten The Chief at His own game? Incredible! Extraordinary!

Faust could see my confusion – and, well, my ignorance of very obscure Welsh history – or was it simply anecdotal folklore? Faust shook his head as if he knew my thoughts and spoke with quiet respect: "The man was named Dafydd Hiraddug and to this day the Welsh mock The Chief with their little ditty:

> Dafydd, Dafydd, badly bred,
> false when living, false when dead.

Signed his soul on Ol' Nick's pact,
but beat The Chief behind His back.

When The Chief pressed His claim
to take that soul that seemed so lame,

Dafydd sent Him back to hell
empty handed, shamed as well.

Dafydd, Dafydd, Welshman's pride,
yes, beat Ol' Nick out for our side.

The Chief hasn't set hoof in Ffinant Trefeglwys, since Dafydd shamed Him there, and He gives the Welsh a wide berth, waits until they've liquored their slick brains and pickled their livers now before making His play."

"Extraordinary."

"Yes, isn't it?"

"So what happened in your case?" I nudged, not wanting to be distracted from the real story, *Faust's* story.

Faust considered my ceiling for some time, its cobwebs, spiders, and centipedes. Then he cleared his throat and launched into a rapid explanation, as if he wanted to get through the material as quickly as possible. "Plan A was simply to refuse to live up to my side of the bargain. After all, I was the one with the power; The Chief was at my beck-and-call, not me at His. However, if for some reason, He had something devious of His own up his sleeve...."

"Yes?"

"Look here: my Plan B was to avail myself of the 'Last Chance Clause' in the enemy's laws."

"The Last Chance Clause? Never heard of it."

"Likely not, but I'm sure you've experienced it," Faust asserted.

"I have?!"

"Yes. At the moment of death, each of us gets one last chance to choose between The Chief and the enemy. The Last Chance Clause has been around forever, but a creepy little tubercular Polish nun re-emphasized it in the first decades of the 20th century."

95

"A NUN?"

"Named *Sister Faustina!*" The bitterness with which Faust uttered that name was palpable, but I couldn't help laughing. In fact, mine was an almost obscene sounding guffaw.

"You got a sister?!" I barked.

"Don't mock me." Faust's tone carried murderous implications. I stifled my laughter and struggled for breath. After a few moments, Faust lit the stub of a tattered half-smoked cigar and drew several lengthy puffs. Then he considered its glowing tip. "After The Chief had trumped me, I asked Him how He voided the Last Chance Clause. Given the fact of it, you and I shouldn't be here. No one should, but The Chief and His original ol' renegades. It was my most bitter moment. The Chief smiled broadly and called His throng around Him. 'Finally!' He crowed, 'Faust speaks! He wants to know how I squelched His Plan B.' Their laughter, wave on wave of it, crushed me and all I could do was stand in humiliated passivity. When silence had fallen, except for a scatter of giggles and chortles, The Chief, to my even greater chagrin, waxed poetic, with a dozen scribes scratching down every word:

> "Well, Faust, I do confess that little nun
> was absolutely right. Confession might
> be good for some souls, but here it only
> gives us heartburn and a bad taste in the mouth.

> "But I digress. She *was* right. Everyone
> at the moment of death has one last chance
> to choose between him or Me, but most –

and here The Chief grinned wickedly and locked His eyes on mine, "*but most*," He repeated for dramatic effect, *'like yourself'* He emphasized with utter contempt for all my sharpness, my worldly wisdom and grand accomplishments, all my supposed power, *'but most'*

> are too damned surprised by the moment –
> or too damned stubborn, or too damned damned
> to take advantage. They're like slinkys.
> You get one started and it'll likely walk

itself all the way downstairs to here. Then
it's 'bye-bye Tweety Bird; hello Sylvester!'
to my Dixie-Land Band's chaotic welcome!"

My "no Plan C, huh?" broke the long ensuing silence.

"No 'C' middle, high, or low," Faust whispered almost to himself.

I don't know what or who got into me at Faust's low point, but I couldn't resist asking, "How did The Chief react? Did He gloat? Or cut a caper? Or simply sneer in your face and mock you?"

Faust gave a long sigh. "The Chief is never so base or unimaginative as to do the expected, but – oh – He did mock me – mocked me in a very quiet, but telling way: He Boxberg Castled me."

"Boxberg Cast...what?!"

"It was a little entertainment I originally dreamed up for all my own so-called friends. I'd been invited to the Castle and was showing off for the low life ladies and lords of the neighborhood. Though it was winter, I dazzled them with sweeping the ground green with fresh spring grasses, and, when they 'ooohed' and 'aaaahed,' I surprised them with platters of all manner of fresh fruit. Apples, pears, delicate raspberries, plums."

"Impressive!"

"But not my point! I turned to some wintering grape vines and, presto, they grew and became pregnant with sweet summer grapes. And as my stupid audience inspected them, I invited them to cut off a bunch and eat – but *not* before I ordered them to do so. Each got his knife and held it against a stem and just as they thought I was going to direct them to 'cut,' I swept away my entire illusion."

"Illusion?"

"Just like The Chief's illusion?"

"Chief's illusion?" I had no idea to what Faust referred, but he ignored my ignorance.

"I swept away the illusion and each idiot found himself holding his knife against the nose of his neighbor. Several of the so-called ladies fainted." Faust chuckled at the memory. "One or two lords winced away their knives so quickly, they inadvertently drew their neighbor's blood, though all the wounds were minor, a nose tip lost here, a split nostril there. The entire party became a sheepish lot of nervous titterers."

I still didn't grasp what all this had to do with The Chief's revenge on Faust and Faust could see my confusion. He growled with impatience: "The Chief drew His knife and held it against His nose for a moment with the cruelest of grins. It was Boxberg all over again, but the trick was on me. It was a figurative, 'Ah! You cut off your nose to spite your face, didn't you?' It was mockery with a fine edge, the ultimate put down."

"Guess you were no Dafydd."

"I'd recommend you shut up: Dafydd, David, Son of David. That name is hated here and should never be openly spoken.

"But," I stammered, trying to change the subject back, "but you'd originally had Him in your power?"

"You just don't get it do you?" Faust spat the comment with acid. It was quite clear there would be no more talking that night and that I would be wise to make myself scarce or wake up later to find a knife at my nose, or worse, my throat.

"Let him wrap himself in his own dark thoughts," I muttered to myself as I closed the door behind me. I'd spend a safer night lurking in the district, keeping to the shadows. It was better to spend the night trying to avoid the open sewers everywhere in the district, than wade any further into Faust's own personal cesspit.

THE HANGING GARDENS

Bunker mentality = an attitude of extreme defensiveness and self-justification based on an exaggerated sense of being under persistent attack from others.

There are some very good reasons to hole up in a bunker. Hitler had his when the Russians entered Berlin. Saddam Hussein had his when the Allies took their wrath out on Baghdad. After the latest sweep by The Chief's press gangs, Faust and I decided we'd run out of reasons to live our lives underground. So one morning – no, it wasn't a fine morning, just a normally wretched, heavily polluted, muggy one – we decided to take the cook's tour of the city's famed and fabled, if somewhat faded, Hanging Gardens! Faded indeed! Everywhere rank vegetation and the overtone buzz and undertone stutter of insects, everywhere the odor of manure, a veritable jungle of grostesque and menacing vegetation – yet strangely attractive to my senses. I examined suppurating buds, the sickening sweet odor of sour-suckle, whole gardens of nightshade, sticky vines that wiggled and writhed like serpents. Odd as it might seem, I felt exhilarated to be away from the cesspits and open sewers of the city, the cramped and gathered buildings piled helter-skelter, until they seemed about to totter toward collapse. The calm here - away from the wails and squeaks of human voices, the demented flow of lies and subterfuges, obscenities and profanities – soothed my rather tense nerves. One could *almost* breathe freely here.

We followed an ancient, unsteady stone wall, until it curved to the left and opened on a large field, acres and acres, dotted with dozens of workers. Each appeared wasted and pained, bent over from too much harvesting, each with a pronounced widow's hump. Each dug and tugged at roots, and one working quite near Faust succeeded in pulling something loose. It shrieked and she toppled over on her backside cursing like a trooper. The root itself lay on the red clay, beating like a living thing, and bleeding.

"Mandrake root harvest." Faust motioned me onward.

We ambled past vast fields of Belladonna. Rows of Venus Fly Traps guarded them against marauding insects. Our tour then seemed to grow less menacing, more pleasant, as we came over a rise and found vast acres of poppies, radiant with color, pods bobbing like so many small somnolent heads. Here and there catatonic addicts sat cross legged, heads bobbing in unison to their pods' motion. Faust's hand swept through a 180 degree arc: "Poppies, coca, marijuana – you want it? All you have to do is ask. If you want, you can stay here almost forever, mindlessly keeping time like a metronomic vegetable."

"Not now," I waved the offer off. "Maybe later." I'd started young at 15 with my first bong full and graduated in my last years to a steady diet of meth. I could hardly remember those vague, early, hazy, lazy days.

We waded on through that psychedelic field of colors. "Hey! W'as up, man!" I looked down into the cloudy eyes of an octogenarian hippie. "Give five!" He held up his foot, rather than the five digits of his right hand. "Hey, man, w'as up?" He repeated as I ignored him and walked on. Yet, I could continue to hear him for some time *Heymanw'asupping.*

Faust tapped his temple and murmured, "Totally burned and blighted. Methinks those six words are all he knows. Look at that clown!" He pointed to another stone head, busily inserting a silk scarf into his left nostril and pulling it out his right. "Coke head idiot! He does that by the hour. Faust stopped in front of the man, nudged his knee, and asked, "Hey, man, w'as up?"

"W'as up, man, w'as up?" came the answer. Faust walked on chuckling to himself murmuring under his breath, *Idiot - mindless and soul-sapped.*" I walked behind him shaken and shaking.

"The next garden is rather exceptional as these things go," Faust announced and hurried me by several fallow fields. We came to a white walled compound and Faust edged its gate open just enough for us to shuffle through sideways. "Keep quiet and you'll hear it soon enough."

Sure enough. As we stood there in silence, a keening sound rose and fell and rose again. The unutterable sorrow in those notes shivered up and down my spine and I glanced at Faust, only to see that he, too, was somewhat disconcerted by it.

He simply motioned for silence and whispered, "keep listening, there's more than keening." I strained to catch more and there was, an undertone of bitter, angry, wrathful voices: male and female voices making horrendous accusations and threats: Screaming profanities, wave upon crashing emotional wave casting up more and more betrayals, humiliations, despair, horror – the hard wrathful voice of hate.

"Come see," he motioned me forward toward a low arch and a second white washed compound. Faust removed a loose stone in the wall and signaled me to take a look.

I was transfixed by the scene before me. Hundreds of harvesters – both male and female - wandering a vast cabbage patch, bending and stooping to retrieve objects from under the fat leaves. Here and there one fetched up something pale or round or elongated like squash and, as she did, she'd wail and drop it into a bloody bag she carried. I gasped and stumbled backward against Faust, when one woman, very near our wall, fumbled under a cabbage plant and drew forth a severed baby's head. A man in a bloody white coat stumbled past, lugging a large garbage can brimming with fetal remains.

"Wha…, wha…, wha…?" Stutter in my shock was all I could do. Then the vast horror of what I was witnessing set in and I sank to the ground.

Faust explained with a tour guide's patter. "Fetal Fields. Unexpectant women and childless men harvesting the remains of their aborted babies – arms, legs, torsos, heads. Little ones sucked apart, dismembered, burned to death with saline solution. When each woman has collected an entire body, she'll stumble to what's called the re-assembly shed at the far end of the field. See? There. Barely visible."

"Looks like a Chicken Coop?"

"Yep, that's it. When she gets there and opens her bloody bag, she finds it empty and gets sent back to search again."

"Then *it's* true," I murmured those three words so low that they were hardly audible, but somehow Faust captured them.

"What's true?"

"That the road to hell is paved with the skulls of un-baptized babies. Must be! All these fetal remains!"

Faust grimaced, "Don't we wish! Nothing would delight The Chief more, but it ain't going to happen."

"Ain't going to?" I stared at him in disbelief, motioning toward the horrors of the fetal fields.

Faust considered his toes protruding from his worn out shoes: "Ain't no babies in hell. The enemy takes them all. Gathers up every last one, like he's the Department of Gift Returns."

"But, but, but…," just then a couple staggered by with a bloody bag.

"It's one of The Chief's charades, a particularly nasty chide, His own mean little comment on what they call *humanity.*"

I stared at Faust in disbelief. "No babies."

"*No* babies," he returned. "Sorry to disappoint you."

"What are the garbage guys doing?"

"Abortion providers," Faust observed without emotion. "Made an industry out of infanticide, filling up trash cans with human remains. Even a few live births ignored and tossed into the medical waste bin. They call this 'healthcare'," he chortled, "'planned parenthood.' The Chief just loves the irony of it all: violates so many of the enemy's key commandments: don't kill, no adultery, don't covet, don't steal."

I got to my feet and stood unsteadily, hoarse, almost speechless. Faust eyed me with condescension and croaked "W'as up, man?" I swayed, near fainting, as one of the women I'd impregnated and for whose abortions I'd paid – thrice! – passed by, then stopped, turned, her face a twisted grimace of bitterness, betrayal, and traumatic abandonment. She seemed to recognize me, but mouthed no name, just "*Why?*" Holding out her gory hands, then stepping forward to grip mine. "*Why? I loved you."* I tried to break away, but she held on: *"Why?"*

Suddenly I felt a rush of anger, the same I felt when I last saw her: "You never loved me. You just couldn't keep your dress down. You're nothing but a cheap whore – always were!" She stumbled backward, as if I'd backhanded her across the face, and I ripped my now bloody hands from her grasp. Then she lunged at my face, hissing, hoping to rake it with her broken, filthy nails, only to be tripped up by Faust, who delivered a swift kick to her abdomen. That doubled her up. He gripped my arm, pulled me away from the scene, and shoved me down the path. "Enough, son, enough. Give her a chance and she'll cut you up and put you in one of her bags."

"She wasn't that bad," I shrugged, "always hot to trot, decent body, good all-round lay. Could I help it she didn't use birth control and wouldn't make me wear a condom?"

"Don't give her a moment's more thought, boy. She was doing five other guys when you knocked her up – just a hot little sexual revolutionary." That stopped me in my tracks, but Faust ignored me, ambled on, and finally I stepped forward to catch up with him.

"Chief calls those fetal fields His 'Secret Garden of Ultimate Sorrows' or something like that!" was Faust's toneless observation. "Or is it 'The Ultimate Garden of Secret Sorrows.' Hmmm! Or maybe 'The Secret Sorrows of the Ultimate Garden'? Whatever!" He shrugged

I refused to glance back at the whitewashed compound, trying to put it out of my mind, until Faust tugged on my arm, turning my aimlessness in a new direction. "Lots of interesting wonders, besides this, to see here. You need to tour 'Predator's Pond.'" He'd suddenly turned upbeat, perhaps to encourage me onward, but it only turned me grayer in the face and more apprehensive as to what might be next.

"'P-P-Predators' P-Pond?" The Gardens were giving me creeps and a definite stutter.

"Some wags around here call it 'Pedophiles' Puddle.' Deep place with lots of thrashing about."

"Thr-thr-thrashing?"

"Pedophiles. Some are disemboweled, filled with stones, and tossed in. Others have millstones tied 'round their necks, and are pushed in. The pond's bottomless. They sink and just keep on sinking, deeper and deeper and deeper. You'll find it interesting."

All I could do was grunt like a distracted pig. "You go on," I pleaded. "I need to sit here on this bench and catch my breath." Even more, I needed time to begin to regain my composure.

"Have it your way." Faust sauntered off and disappeared into a large copse. I breathed easier just having him gone for a spell and I began to look around. I'd no intention of going anywhere near that white walled compound again or of seeking out *Predators' Pond.* I turned down a path that appeared to hold nothing ominous.

Path turned on path and soon I was hedged in. This section of the Gardens appeared to be an elaborate medieval maze and soon I was feeling both lost and yet drawn on. Trees in the distance seemed festooned with what appeared to be large clumps of hanging mosses, like the cypresses found in Southern swamps – except this part of the Garden wasn't swampy. It was simply still. Deathly still. No insect murmur. No skitter of creatures in the underbrush. If I didn't know better, I'd have thought I wandered into cemetery, a strange, totally silent memorial garden.

Yet, I found the quiet soothing my drawn and quartered nerves and wandered on without any goal in mind. I wanted to find a secluded niche down some almost hidden side path, sink down on a bench and calmly contemplate. I found that side path and was brought up against a dead end, a garden niche with a copse of stunted and gnarled trees, leafless and scarred by multiple lightning strikes, burned black, a jagged splay of grasping branches etched more darkly into the gloom than I thought possible. I wandered in among them, feeling my way gingerly, careful to watch where I set my feet, handing myself from tree to tree. And then I stumbled head long and face first into a hanging corpse, eyeless, face blue-black. The rope tight around the neck had cut deep. How long those tattered, torn remains had hung there was beyond telling.

"*Aauugh!*" I reeled backwards and stumbled into a second body, whirled in heart-stopping fright, and found myself face-to-face with Faust. "*You!*"

"Yes. Me. They don't call these the city's Hanging Gardens for nothing, do they?" He spat on the ground below the rotting corpse and surveyed its emaciated and desiccated limbs like a doctor examining a patient. He turned and smiled wickedly at me, as if he'd read my thoughts. "Professional interest. Remember, I'm a doctor and play one here." Faust caressed the scarred bark of the tree, studied it even more closely than the corpse, then tapped it with his finger and looked at me: "The Tree of the Knowledge...?"

"Damn the tree!" I shuddered. "Who...?" I pointed at the corpse. The atmosphere was becoming so oppressive here that I kept gagging on my words.

"You know the old song, *John Brown's Body Lies A-rottin' in the Grave?*"

"*That's* John Brown?!"

"No, stupid. That's Judas a-hanging in his tree. Filthy little traitor," Faust observed without anger or any other emotion. "At least that's what the old shout-and-denouncers call him, and rather unfairly too."

Dazed as I was, I allowed Faust to lead me back up the path away from the niche, "Judas? You *joke*," I managed to cough out the three words.

"Place of honor at the very center of the Gardens, though I can't see why. You never saw a man make such a muck of betrayal as Iscariot did!"

"Jud.., Filth…, Traitor, HERE!" I was still having trouble controlling my tongue.

"Judas was an honorable man, just as we are all, all, honorable men." Faust's histrionic tone annoyed me in the extreme.

"You're as daft as a duck!" I'd finally found my voice.

"No, no. I understand him better than most." Faust could see I was completely incredulous. He guided me to a park bench and we sat down. I could see he'd grown more subdued, more serious. "He *was* honorable as he was able. Problem was he was hardly able and he failed to understand that. You *all* fail to grasp that – all except that uncanny Nazarite. He seemed to have no illusions at all."

"Nazarite…?"

Faust ignored my question and plunged on: "Judas wasn't quite right nor quite wrong, neither thoroughly good nor evil, but in a muddle like the rest of us: a tangle of good intentions and bad judgments, high ideas and base desires. Those latter hang about you all like so many loose threads. Start to tease them and the whole garment begins to unravel."

"But the money! The money he took!" I objected.

"Now let's not be stupid," Faust stung me. "Judas didn't seek his job. The Nazarite and his disciples needed a money man. Not Matthew, the tax collector. Too much temptation for him, and not one of the Zealots either who might be tempted to make unapproved and compromising political contributions. They picked Judas just because money *wasn't* his weakness, whatever the Nazarite's gossips claim. He accounted for every penny, no, never pinched a single coin of all that passed his hands. And don't call that silver a money grab! It didn't mean a shekel to him; it was simply a means to an end."

"That's hard to believe," I observed tonelessly. "Very hard to believe."

"No. Not at all. It's easy to believe he took the money, when you consider the people who offered him the bribe wouldn't believe he had more high tone motives. Look. I know him better than anyone else, except perhaps The Chief. Believe me, his problems were far more complicated than simple lucre. He was higher minded than most around here. His job became him or shall we say he became the job. The more he succeeded, the more he craved success. He was the one who made things happen, who worked the crowds, cared for the poor, the blind, the lame, and deaf. He graced every table with food, including the Passover meal. But after early success, opposition set in. The Nazarite's ministry crested and went into decline. Revenues dropped and Judas heard some complain about what he'd done with the funds, though he'd accounted for everything. The real problem was that followers were dropping away from all the Nazarite's talk of arrest and crucifixion, death and burial. And that perturbed even the almost imperturbable Judas."

Faust eyed me to assess if I was buying his explanation. I had to admit, it sounded plausible. Faust could see he'd gained a foothold and went on: "Remember Mary with her pint of nard anointing the Nazarite's feet at Lazarus' house? Remember Judas' reaction? *Why wasn't this sold and the money given to the poor?* Don't be fooled! The poor weren't his concern. He could no longer see and appreciate the most simple and sincere acts of love. I think that's when the Nazarite read him and knew Judas would betray him. What I can't understand is why the Nazarite never took action to get rid of him."

"Some whisper Judas wanted to provoke his Nazarite to seize heaven's throne and earth. Others claim disillusionment, bitterness: that Judas aimed to retrieve something from the debacle the Nazarite had brought, say silver or simple revenge. But I'm not sure he understood anything. He felt he'd become the indispensable make-it-happen man. When the Nazarene whispered, *Do what you must do and quickly,* Judas straightway went and did it! He took action whatever the outcome. Let's leave him alone to sort it all out."

"Sort it all out?!" I blurted. "The man's dead and rotting! How's he supposed to sort anything out?"

Faust looked into the distance. "Dead. Dead and partly dead. Dead as you but not dead. Dying but never quite dead. Rotten as a fallen apple, perhaps, and quite wormy, but still contemplating himself, even from his present vantage – or maybe we should call it his disadvantage - point."

"What nonsense," I murmured mostly to myself.

"Nonsense? Perhaps. Babble? Perhaps. But there are more things in this world than your feeble mind can grasp." That I was almost willing to grant. I'd been learning much and sensed I'd still much to learn.

However, I wasn't about to let Faust have the satisfaction of checkmating my argument. "Never no mind," Faust continued, "Let's leave him alone. It's his to sort out. He doesn't need anyone but himself. Come to think of it, he doesn't *have* anyone but himself. The Romans trusted only their own, and his priestly allies abandoned him, and he put the Nazarite's forgiving folk in a most unforgiving mood. And The Chief?"

"Yes," my interest was piqued, "What about The Chief?"

"The Chief had no further use for him."

Faust paused and I confess I was ready to leave Judas alone, leave the Gardens alone too. Enough of Gardens. They were noxious plots of riddles and horrors, graves and nightmares. "Let's get back to the bunker." It was more of a plea on my part than a command.

"Suit yourself," Faust shrugged and ambled toward the exit.

I followed like a bitten puppy, totally empty.

NORMALITY'S INSTABILITY

*"There is Babylon…and here is building up and throwing down continually. She builds,
the spirit of the Lord confounds, then down goes her building; then up with another, then down again.
Thus is her course without end, when the spirit of the Lord disturbs her.*
-Isaac Penington

We tramped along one of the wider thoroughfares. It was nowhere near as grand as The Chief's Boulevard, but traffic – motor and foot – moved along at an acceptable rate. Problem was: Acceptable rate was never acceptable to Faust. We had traveled across several districts to get to the Gardens, and the way back was proving long, tiresome, and at best circuitous. Impatient with our progress as usual, Faust, with his intimate knowledge of Babylonia, knew a multitude of shortcuts and he led me up one maze of streets and alleys, some barely wide enough for us to pass through walking side-by-side, and then down through byways that I'd never seen before. If he wanted to lose me, tonight was his night to do so, because I began to feel like a very small rodent in a near infinite maze. We passed from a particularly seedy, decrepit district and entered what appeared to be an upscale neighborhood, one with wider streets and less confusion, less confusion until Faust suddenly stopped stark still, cocked his head, and listened intently.

"What...?" I barely whispered.

"SHHH!" He shushed me with such force, I hushed.

In the next second, he motioned me forward, "Hurry. Hurry!" I stepped up my pace, but insisted on knowing, "Why? More patrols or bounty hunters?" I glanced about, surveyed the shadows doorways were becoming, but could see nothing menacing.

"This neighborhood's dangerous and, if we don't get out of here soon, we never will." Instead of goading me forward, Faust's comment actually stopped me in my tracks.

"Dangerous? How? Looks like one of the better neighborhoods I've seen, none of the usual transients and riff-raff on the streets." I hadn't a clue what Faust was talking about. I looked from building to building, some small and squalid, others elegant and rising dozens of stories, and recognized the district – The Aquarian Borough, known all over the city as one of the more desirable areas, blocks upon blocks of expensive townhouses and condominiums, accommodations sought after by those hoping to ladder up. Restaurants and boutiques catered to needs here, rather than the back street bars, seedy crack houses, and brothels of the bunker district in which we hid. There actually seemed some planning to the district, but over time units had been converted, floors and new wings added in a disconcerting hodge-podge until the design of entire blocks disappeared into a chaos of stairways, jutting levels, false walls, and uncertain foundations. Someone had given way to the temptation for rampant development and, within a few years, the entire district had become overbuilt. "Unfettered growth to meet a burgeoning population and its demands," was how any district manager often described it with a shrug of his shoulders. And if pressed on his neglect of building standards, he would bitterly complain of the quotas he was forced to meet and the influx of more souls to house every week.

Though my question about danger was innocent enough, Faust wheeled on me with a ferocious glare. He held up his hand for silence and whispered, "Listen!"

I stood still and listened. Nothing. Well, not nothing: Somewhere several stories above us the muted noise of a rather raucous party filtered down – the high pitched shrieks and overwrought giggling of drunken women, pulsing chaotic music, punctuated by occasional profanities and shattering glass. And over to the left, from the deep throat of an alley, angry curses rose – two men having it out over...? I looked at Faust. "The party? Or the fight?"

"No, stupid!" He slapped me up the side of my head.

"Hey! Ow! What...!?" Faust shoved me against a wall pushing the side of my face against its rough surface with a hold so strong I couldn't break it. "Listen! Just shut up and listen! You'll hear it."

My ear, pressed painfully to the wall, began to pick up something – a deep distant groaning, as if from the very bowels of the earth, then closer the snap of – I glanced sideways at Faust – "wood cracking?" The next second my ear caught the sound of small pieces of plaster falling between the walls – sporadic rather than the thunderous rush like one would hear if an entire wall were collapsing. Faust released his pressure and I shook myself out of his grasp. "So?" I hissed, rubbing my scraped ear.

"We need to move much faster than we are. This area's long overdue."

"Overdue?"

"Unsteady. Far too long. The entire district's under stress and those stresses must be near the breaking point."

I felt like an idiot in an echo chamber, but couldn't help it. I'd no idea what Faust was talking about, but at that very moment, almost as if to punctuate his observation, I heard a shot, like a nail snapping under great pressure. In the next nanosecond, Faust was on the move down the street faster than I'd ever seen him move. He'd succeeded in spooking me and I nodded, "Yes. Let's get."

We hurried deeper into the maze of alleyways. "Shortcut here!" Faust pointed down a wide thoroughfare as we emerged from the narrowest ones. For the twisted, humped creature he'd become, Faust moved with surprisingly quickness, using a half rolling, half lumbering gallop, reminiscent of the one the hunchback of Notre Dame utilized. A cadaverous figure turned off the thoroughfare into the alley at the very moment we burst out: "Hey, mates! What's the hurry? You in trouble?"

Faust pushed him roughly aside with a brusque, "No! You are!" And I bolted by him without a sideways glance or apology.

"Why you...," he let loose with a torrent of the most vile curses I'd heard in years, extraordinary because I'd become so used to hearing torrents of curses. I'd almost become deaf to them.

I was about to turn around and hurtle a few choice ones of my own, when Faust grabbed my shoulder and nearly pulled me over in his attempt to keep me moving. "He'll get his," Faust hissed between breathless gasps, "if what I think happens."

We were nearly to The Chief's great Boulevard, when I felt the ground tremble under my feet and saw Faust stumble too and double step to keep from falling. The earth under our feet gave a low throated groan followed by several heavy thuds that seemed to come from everywhere at once. Faust and I both turned about at the same second and saw it – the entire district shuddered and began a slow motion rolling collapse – slow at first, but gaining tidal wave like speed as it moved toward us. A second wave, a cacophony of sound blew over us – a chaos of shrieking timbers, the fireworks of transformer explosions, rows of towering light standards dropping straight earthward in unison, and the terrified screams of hundreds, perhaps thousands of souls. And then we saw it: the great rolling, billowing cloud of debris and dust sweeping toward us. "Run!" Faust nearly deafened me with his own roar to be heard over the pandemonium. And he loped with amazing speed as I dashed after him toward the open door of a bar and grill near the Boulevard. We fell through the door way together and kicked the door shut behind us just as the great black menace of the debris cloud swept the street.

"Good timin', fellas," the place was empty except for the bartender, a man with a face that looked like skin stretched on skull and jaw bones. "Aquarian finally go? Sounds like it."

Faust got to his feet first, brushing himself off. "Aquarian it was. The whole district just folded up and fell." We could hear sirens now, distant, but headed our direction, a steady stream of wailings rising steadily in decibels. We'd soon have to shout to hear one another.

"Fires already got a good start, I wager," The bartender had a voice like ground glass on porcelain, one that sent shivers up and down my spine.

Faust nodded: "Be smelling roasted flesh for weeks. Better roasted, I guess, than rotten."

"It's the scree-reams of the livin' caught in the ruins by them flames that raises my hair," the bartender swept his hand across his bald head. "How 'bout a drink? We're all gonna need some soon to keep our throats clear and our minds together." Faust readily agreed and I was more than ready for some liquid, my throat dry as sandpaper from our mad, frightful flight here.

"Third dis-rict down this dic-aid," the bartender slurped his drink down in the very act of speaking. "The great fire on Nero Heights first, then the collapse of the entire Ambrosia Springs development, and now the Aquarian!"

"You mean this has happened before?!" I looked from our barman to Faust, horrified at the very thought that what I'd just experienced was an almost regular event.

They gazed at me as if I was daft. Then the barman glanced at Faust: "He's new here, right?"

"Newest of the new, you might say," Faust returned with a wink and both of them chortled. "Yes, newest of the new!" They both raised their glasses in a mock toast to me. I flushed a dark crimsoned, thankful that the lighting in the bar was so poor they couldn't see how thoroughly flustered I was. In the next seconds, flashing lights and raging sirens momentarily blinded and deafened us as an armada of fire engines roared past raising more clouds of dust and headed down the thoroughfare up which we'd come. As the sirens waned with distance, a second armada of vehicles – pick-up trucks, vans, jalopies, thundered past.

Faust guffawed: "There they go! Never far behind – The Chief take the hindmost!"

"Who?" I knew I shouldn't have asked.

"Looters, dummy. Who would you expect?"

I shrugged and shut up. In the silence, we listened to the powerful roar and bark of the flames, the occasional staccato of rapid fire explosions punctuated by further sounds of collapse. The barkeep eyed us both: "I'd better close up, boys. No tellin' how far the fires will spread. Suggest you head out too – at least if you're not Aquarians."

"No sir, we are not," Faust returned with the definiteness of an injured man that anyone would presume so. He slapped some coins down for our drinks. The barkeep scooped and pocketed them, conveniently ignoring the fact that Faust had overpaid him. I was about to call it to his attention, but caught Faust's "no, boy" glance as I opened my mouth. I bit my tongue instead.

We made fast tracks, putting the Aquarian far behind us. I glanced once or twice over my shoulder as we mounted a rise in the road. The Borough was "fully involved" as fire authorities would describe it, a veritable firestorm lighting up other districts for miles around. We found it difficult for a time to make headway against the near hurricane force inrush of air to feed the flames. "That firestorm's so intense, the entire neighborhood will be ashes and dust tomorrow," Faust observed drily. After we'd gained sufficient distance, we decided to sit out the commotion in another bar a couple of miles distant. Traffic died to a trickle about 4 a.m. and, when I glanced out the door, though the fire continued to burn hot, it had lost much of its initial superheat and all-consuming violence. It was not that the fire companies had done great work. They hadn't. Whole teams of first and second responders had succumbed to the conflagration, and simply added themselves as additional fuel for the flames. The looters, a tad wiser in their greed, lost fewer of their number, but found only thin pickings on the periphery of the disaster

Faust and I continued our passage back to our bunker and as we walked for some time silently, but in step, I felt I must have an answer to my unanswered question: "This happens…often? Regularly? Well, almost so?"

"Not every day," he returned. "Not even every year, but at least once or two times in a decade – three's a bit startling. But the Aquarian district was long, long overdue. I hesitated to take us through there tonight for that very reason, but it was the best shortcut back to our bunker and it had stood so long that it didn't seem that much of a risk until…."

"Until?"

"Until I saw one of the tallest buildings had shifted so dramatically and had such an ominous lean to it that I realized some sort of collapse was imminent – and once it went, it'd take down the entire district. Remember when I asked you to listen?"

I rubbed my bruised and scraped ear, "Do I."

"I caught the increasing sound of crumbling plaster falling between the walls, and – my ears are as sensitive as a dog's ears – I could catch the squeaking and moaning deep in that pile of buildings – could hear that very subtle, but very ominous shifts were happening. I realized that my seemingly benign little gamble was turning into a disaster for us and that's when I shouted 'run!'"

I'm sure Faust caught me eying him with doubt, but he ignored it. As we turned the corner to our bunker, I scanned the buildings around me. Everything looked reasonably stout and tidy – worn and dirty and a tad overbuilt and under supported, but still pretty four-square and sturdy – lots better built that the Aquarian district had appeared. I breathed easier.

"Oh, it'll happen someday here too." Had Faust read my mind? His flat statement caught me so completely by surprise that I couldn't find words to respond. "And the Aquarian area will be rebuilt, and then overbuilt, developed into a creeping disaster, and someday it'll happen there again – many, many years hence, of course." He was so matter-of-fact that I could only stare. "As wonderful, special, lovely and well-designed as some parts of the city seem, all of Babylonia's neighborhoods are growing towards future collapses. Babylonia's like California or Japan or some parts of China, always unsteady, shifting, shaking, and on occasion crashing. It's the nature of the place. You might call it normality's instability."

"Wh-wh-why?" My dazed stutter.

"Bad ground? Bad foundation, maybe? Who knows? Just the nature of the place, I guess. It's a shape shifting world," Faust shrugged and opened the door to the steps down to our rooms. I could see from his nod that I'd get no more of an answer than that, though I believe he knew more than he was telling me.

THE MYSTERY OF MYSTERIES

"Kill God and he'll mock you, because he won't stay dead."

We had barely thrown the bolt to our secure little bunker when I noticed a small white square of paper and snatched it up. "Come immediately! *Stopheles*" was all that was scrawled on it. Had it just arrived? Or been sitting about all day and night?

Faust didn't help. "Better get crackin'," he advised. "I'm sure you're way late."

"Thanks!"

"Don't mention it."

"What do you think this kind of summons means?"

"Must be getting near the end of the matriculation process," he shrugged, giving me no more encouragement than before. "Each summons gets more preemptory than the last as you get closer to the end."

"The end?"

"You ask way, way, too many questions. Let's leave it. Get on your way, if you know what's good for you."

~~~~~

I arrived at the compound with some trepidation, but found, not devastation or a mock Jerusalem this time, but a magnificent hybrid of Beijing's Forbidden City, Moscow's Kremlin, and the District of Columbia's sprawling Federal complex. I found myself passed along quickly by the guards, as if they had orders to speed up the schedule, until I stood at the great bronze double doors of Stopheles' chambers. I fully expected the door to swing open when I knocked and that I would be greeted by Stopheles, though with what demeanor I hesitated to guess. Imagine my surprise when an unfamiliar voice boomed, *"Entrée vous!"* A servant?

I touched the latch and the heavy door swung open to reveal a short, very stout, yea huge – no, *gargantuan* - woman in a bulky blue cotton

Mao-like uniform with a Colonel's insignia. A little over five feet tall, she must have weighed 400 to 500 pounds. *How many stones is that?* My mind asked, thinking back to the old English weight system. Yes, *stone* seemed a better measure. She certainly looked like a great boulder.

The room seemed much larger than when I'd visited Stopheles there. Perhaps it was the lack of furniture and decoration. The room now held only a common wooden desk and chair, rather distressed and shabby, none of the treasures, the grand tapestries, leather furniture, and crystal chandeliers that Stopheles would admire as he circled the chamber, caressing an item here, hefting a vase or statue there, sweeping his fingers over the printed page of a fantastically illuminated manuscript.

"Sto-Sto-pheles?" was all I could stutter as I leaned back and checked the door, thinking I'd grossly erred and come to the wrong office. No. It was the same chamber I'd met Stopheles in. The woman didn't even look up, just curtly commanded, "Come!" She continued to focus on something on the desk before her, but beckoned me forward with her left hand, then held it out. "Coin!" I still had my duplicate copper coin along with the fool's gold Caligula piece in my pocket and decided to see if I could get by with the former. I dropped it in her upturned palm. Without examining it, she opened an empty desk drawer and tossed it in, where it spun and clattered. With one swift ham-handed slap, she banged the drawer closed like a pistol shot. She still had not glanced up, but now snapped, "No Stopheles tonight! You're seeing Bēel! Second door on your left!" I dearly wanted to ask what had happened to Stopheles, but her manner brooked no lingering. Her whole tone shouted "Get the lead out, Buster!" I was tempted to apologize for my lateness, suspecting it as the cause of her abruptness. Something in the deep recesses of my mind whispered, *don't ask, no apology, don't say anything,* and though I hadn't the tiniest fact on which to hang my suspicion, I still wondered if she was some kind of Stopheleon joke.

As I entered the second door on the left, the creature that rose to greet me must have only been three foot seven. His huge – I can only describe them as - "bug eyes" searched me for several seconds. Then seemingly satisfied, he extended a gnarled hand – a fist really, the fingers turned in as if he had a case of crippling arthritis. I touched it gingerly and nodded, and he in turn motioned me to follow him to yet another door. He took out a large ring of keys – enough keys it seemed to lock or open all the cell doors of all the world's prisons. We proceeded down a dim hallway to another door, and another, and another. Each Bēel unlocked, then relocked tight behind us. The air grew musty and stale and I began to feel somewhat asthmatic and struggled increasingly to gulp full breaths of air. I was about to hyperventilate, when we reached the last door and bug-eyes turned to me, "You must *never, on pain of oblivion*, speak of what you're about to see." Those eyes searched mine.

I drew a deep breath and murmured, "I will *never* speak of it."

Bug-eyes nodded and inserted a skeleton key. The mechanism ground metal-on-metal from lack of use, and threw the bolt with a dead "thunk." He motioned me ahead into the darkness beyond and switched on a dim blue luminary which bathed the place in glacial light. The room was large and a curtain covered most of one wall. Bug-eyes threw a switch and an electric motor creaked, ground, and squealed, opening the curtain by jerks and starts, starts and jerks. The wall held an immense painting, a vast desert wilderness scene. As I strained my eyes to see better, the scene began to glow as with increasingly harsh sunlight – but sunlight not coming from any window or spotlight, but from the painting itself. Soon I was squinting. Bug-eyes had turned his back on the thing with a grimace of terrible distaste.

Then I saw it – a small figure, a man, in the lower right climbing and descending over the wasted terrain, pausing often in what seemed to be prayer or meditation. He was young, but not too young – mid- to late-twenties, perhaps thirty at most.

"You're relieved Bēel!" **Stopheles!** I nearly jumped out of my skin, not having heard him come in. Bēel bowed and began an obsequious retreat, but not so quickly that my ears failed to catch his parting exhalation about the "blasphemous obscenity" we were viewing. I turned to Stopheles, but he rather sternly motioned my attention back to the painting – if I may call it that. It was the strangest painting I'd ever seen - the harsh desert light, the moving figure, and now a second, a shadow stalking some ways behind. No, I wasn't viewing static art, but I'm uncertain to this day what it might have been. We watched the first figure, Stopheles with a look of sick distaste for what was happening.

The man. We watched him sift over the sand shunting down valleys, contemplating clouds and their old absolution. We watched as he studied the strange case of his flesh, its rage at old wrong, all the hoarse and violent voices within him – those that mourn and are not comforted, the death of meekness, the unattainable earth, the merciful doubting their mercy, men who revile and persecute and utter all manner of evil falsely for their own sakes.

Then the slither of sand over sand stilled.

The stalker stepped flagrant as God from the silent stone. Their long guarded truce had ended. How many years had it been?

The man already knows how it will be: the common confusion of voices easy and quite believable, the wild beating screams shaking the earth; the struggle wider than the world, longer than time; the ancient and invertebrate hatred that will stalk him down his days. He doesn't even consider the stones it sets before him like so many loaves, but breaks his fast with the simplest words, *Man does not live by bread alone.*[5]

Stopheles groaned from what must have been an intense inward pang or pain. After a moment, he lifted his head and motioned to an invisible technician, who dimmed the lights slowly back to cold blue. Then Stopheles motioned me abruptly toward the door. He could see my quizzical look as we stepped into the hall, my mystification over the whole experience. "You haven't a clue what you just witnessed?" His tone was dead level.

"No. Not a clue." Yet, I felt comprehension danced like an itching irritation just beyond my mental fingertips. I was overwhelmed by the feeling that I'd seen something of immense significance, but something in me screamed: *keep it to yourself!* I said no more.

"Good. The scene is called *The Mystery*. I don't understand it either." Stopheles smiled thinly, not warmly. "Don't bother yourself with it. You *shouldn't* understand it, if you get my drift. Even The Chief often comes here and broods over it. Then He's testy as hell for nights afterward. It has that impact on us." I nodded that I could understand that, even given my own neophyte circumstances. Comprehension danced like an itching irritation just beyond my mental fingertips.

Instead of my usual immediate dismissal, Stopheles guided me back through the halls to his chambers. "Whiskey?" He'd opened the bar.

"I thought you only drank brandy or the finest wines."

"We need something stronger after that little scene. Whiskey will wash away the rancid taste of that outrageous grotesque." He grinned as he poured mine, but it was a grin without warmth. Perfunctory. Subtly insincere.

We downed a shot each, then another, then a third. My head began to swim and Stopheles himself began loosening up. I steeled myself against the moment he might begin another strip tease or urinate on himself again. He seemed to want to talk and after two or three shots more, he was almost babbling. "We never understood what went wrong. Forty days without food. The bread should have worked!" I hadn't a clue what he was referring to, but his tone carried the unmistakable undertone of indignation.

"You've read The Chief's *Satanic Sorrows*, correct?" Stopheles caught me out as he whirled on me, dropping his self-absorbed meditation.

"I, I, well, yes, you gave me a copy." It was a flimsy and obvious lie. Fool that I was, I still had not read it. Stopheles eyed me as if he knew the truth, but rather than pounce, chose to educate me by his own dramatic recitation of one of The Chief's laments.

"The Chief captured our whole confusion in the little book. Listen up!" Stopheles ordered.

> "Rock, scissors, paper! None of it worked!
> We were sure he'd lay hands on those stones,
> especially since he was so hungry.
> *Stones to bread*, I'd whispered, *Nothing*
> *to stub your toe on there!* But he didn't buy a crumb!
>
> Now the temple's pinnacle – that was a long shot.
> *I* wouldn't have jumped, 'cause I don't like the angels
> who'd come to catch me (if any came at all).
> He didn't jump at that either. Not even tempted!
> But all the world's kingdoms! They usually
>
> work like charms and should have turned his head.
> Maybe I was a tad too eager, the pushy salesman
> sensing he's close to a sale. Wish I would
> have crooned, "All the world's kingdoms?
> I'll let you sleep on that and come back tomorrow.

I'll bring more stones for you to touch."

Stopheles studied his empty glass with marked distaste for what seemed an age, then turned his gaze on me – a hard, bitter, cruel gaze. As his eyes bored into me, I grew nervous, fidgety, uncertain whether I should speak or excuse myself. The more he stared, the more I sensed his utter hatred – at me? Or some unexpressed, unexplained.... Then Stopheles' lips moved, but what he said was inaudible.

"What?" I thought I'd better ask, rather than sitting mum as a fool. Asking might break his glare.

"*GET OUT!*" He roared and I rocketed out of my chair toward the door. "Get the hell out of my sight! I've had more than enough of you and everyone else!" As the door slammed behind me, I leaned against it to catch my breath, which came in huge gasps. This was a Stopheles I'd never seen before and never wanted to see again: a dangerous Stopheles, a Stopheles with deadly intent. I staggered past his strange receptionist, making a wide circuit around her desk, lest she mete out some form of her own rough justice to follow-up Stopheles' ejection. I exited the compound, hurried across the grand parade ground and headed down toward the city triple time. The guards watched me go, some amused, some bemused, all of them as uncaring as always.

IN THE GREAT HALL OF PETITE CHIEFS

'...Babylon the Great! She has become a home for demons and a haunt for every evil spirit,
a haunt for every unclean and detestable bird. For all the nations have
drunk the maddening wine
of her adulteries. The kings of the earth committed adultery with her, and the
merchants of the earth
grew rich from her excessive luxuries.
-Rev.18:2-3

I spent days hiding out in the bunker after the shock of my last meeting with Stopheles, mystified both by his mystery and by his shape-shifting character, what seemed his manic-depressive tendencies. A session like that can leave one shaken and uncertain to the core, awaiting retribution, fearing what form it might take. Over a week later, the pall of that meeting had only begun to dissipate, when it reasserted itself with the arrival of another summons from the Central Compound.

Another educational tour? Not another mystery! Please! My hope was that this particular session would be with The Chief, but, no. When I arrived I was directed to Stopheles' chambers as was becoming usual. I don't know what it is, but my conferences with him appeared to be progressively deteriorating, each one less stimulating, more troublesome, more marred by insinuations or threats, than the session before. Was it something about me? Some emerging flaw of mine? Or the weight of business upon him? Or simply the old adage: "Familiarity breeds contempt." Perhaps for Stopheles, it did. Intelligent men and women usually have a very low regard for those around them.

After viewing *The Mystery* and receiving the brunt of Stopheles' sudden explosive anger, I had no real desire to see him again, in fact, feared another summons from him or his Colonel. However, while I could fear the summons and wince at its brief and preemptory tone, I knew I could not ignore it. Running and hiding were not options. One might be able to run in The Chief's domain but I suspected wherever I hid, I'd be ferreted out sooner or later. No. Without an exit, one has no escape. Ignoring the summons was impossible. I knew I had to report, whatever consequences awaited me.

What awaited me was the Colonel.

She appeared all spit-and-polish, greeted me in a Waffen-SS uniform, complete with steel toed jack boots, and red swastika armband. Before I could say anything, she stopped her work, marched to the door of Stopheles' chamber, entered, saluted him with a "Heil Hitler, your appointment *Ubergruppenführer!*" The Stopheles that stood behind the desk stunned me once more with his appearance. He stood every inch a doppelganger for Heinrich Himmler, right down to the Reichsführer SS-uniform, mousy mustache and rimless glasses.

He stepped from behind his desk, circled me with his hands behind his back, glanced at the Colonel and purred, "What do you think, Colonel? A perfect Waffen recruit or what?"

She responded with a curt, "Umph! Worthless for anything but boot leather I'd say." She clicked her heels with another "Heil Hitler" and left the room.

"Well, now," Stopheles, an eyebrow cocked, responded softly, "Guess we won't put you in *her* unit."

At that moment, I found my tongue and stammered, "W-w-w-h-h-at unit is that, sir?"

"Never no mind. That's not why you're here. We're not into the Night of the Long Knives or *Kristallnacht* – just a special visit to a very special place."

"P-p-place, sir? And the uniform, sir?" Visions of the nightmares at Dachau and Auschwitz gripped my heart. Was that where I was headed?

Stopheles smiled broadly: "Just celebrating *Der Führer's* birthday!"

"The Chief's? The Chief had a birth day??"

"No, no, no, no. My, you are easily confused!"

"It's a confusing place, sir."

"Indeed it is, and by design, but that's neither here nor there. Come!"

Stopheles' orders were orders and I followed them. We marched down a long marble hallway, him humming an old Wehrmacht marching song, until he halted in front of a door marked, *Petite Chiefs*, fished a golden key from his pocket, and unlocked it. Garish red lamps along the long hall's length flicked on when the door swung open and I saw both walls were studded with small four-by-four inch portraits. "Our Chief's hall of honor for all those petite chiefs who would follow in His footsteps!" He waved me ahead of him with a flourish and entered what I can only describe as the *scarlet realm*. I began examining the portraits, not dozens nor hundreds, but *thousands!* Some visages had faded and become almost indistinguishable. Others, though clear and named, were not readily identifiable, at least to me. Who was Papa Doc or Noriega or Pol Pot? But, yet, here was Ghengis Khan, a host of Chinese emperors and Japanese warlords, Rameses II, Julius Caesar, Tiberius, Caligula, Vlad Dracula the Impaler. The hall and its lines of portraits seemed to be pointed toward infinity, there were so many! Franco, Mussolini, Kaiser Wilhem, Lenin, Stalin…and finally, Adolf Hitler in a five-by-seven portrait. It departed enough from the size of the others that I turned questioningly to Stopheles. He simply murmured, "He's *just* a tad special."

"A tad?"

"Yes, he's really *not* that special, but he saw, to Our Chief's delight, the true nature of racism, and, more, its great potential, a potential we've not yet even begun to realize!"

"But racism is as old as the human race," that was obvious and I probably needn't have stated it.

"Ah!" Stopheles raised his forefinger, "Yes! But it's not about color."

"It isn't?"

"And it's not about blood, though ol' Adolf thought it was and spilled enough of it!"

"It isn't?" I felt a dozen times a dunce, having no idea where Stopheles was going with his explanation and Stopheles was considering me with the gaze of a schoolmaster, the gaze of one considering whether he should cane his worst pupil. Then he relented, sighed.

"Think about it, son. Think about it." I thought about it, thought hard, but came up blank. "Who did Hitler and Himmler send to the gas chambers?"

"Well, Jews, of course." But the obvious was not what Stopheles was obviously angling for.

"And?"

"Russians?"

"And?"

"Poles?"

"<u>And</u>? Keep going, son. Be expansive!"

"Slavs, semites, gypsies, homosexuals, the mentally retarded…."

"Yes! Now you're on the way," Stopheles beamed at me, as if I'd finally become a somewhat apt pupil, an impression I promptly ruined.

"On my way where?"

"To the heart and soul of what racism is! Is it *that* hard to figure out? Your mind is dominated by skin color, blood. That's not what racism is all about! NOT IN THE LEAST!" Stopheles thundered at me, exercised near violence by my obtuseness, my ignorance, while I foundered helplessly, having no idea what he was trying to get me to see. I was back in First Grade and Sister Angela was bearing down on me with her metal ruler, about to strike more than fear in me. I, the whelp, went home each night with welts!

Stopheles, to calm himself, took off his rimless glasses, cleaned them with considerable care while I considered the condition of the toes of my shoes, and then: "Let's try this from another direction. I'm about to execute a thousand men, women, and children for mein Führer. How can I do that? I'm a human being."

I chirped the easy answer: "Orders are orders!"

Stopheles' color rose. "Yes, but that's only a small part of it. Some will balk at such orders. Many might only obey and tepidly so for self-preservation, but to do it willingly, patriotically, day-after-day, on an industrial, dis-assembly line basis, how could you do *that?* You could do that only if....?"

Final exam time! I knew the next answer I'd better get right: "I could only do that if....if....if...they weren't human beings?" It wasn't an outright answer, more the poor student's guess, but it satisfied my instructor.

"Yes! Hitler and Himmler were able to recruit such willing workers, because those workers were convinced that the people they disposed of were *not human.* That's the only way you can get people to commit the most unspeakable crimes. What did Herr Hitler teach: 'there's a little bit of me in every one.' Yes! Some dark seed of murder and destruction that the whole human race has become prone to, Cain's nature! Some genocidal tendency that can turn well meaning, ordinary men and women into mass murderers. Men and women who can return home at night to a most mundane life with their wives, husbands, and children, after a day of gassing and murdering tens of thousands of their brethren. The key to this ability is..."

I'd got it! "In the belief that the people you're killing are not truly human, but a lower species, vermin, infidels, mentally defective, sick, worthless, evil."

Stopheles beamed: "Now you've got it."

"But wasn't this aberration limited to Hitler?"

"No. Definitely not! Consider the Communists who liquidated millions of people, because those people were of a different economic class, therefore evil and unredeemable: *sub-human*. Or radical Islamists who have divided the world into faithful Muslims and infidels. Or Hutus and Tutsis who slaughter one another, because they're from different tribes. Or Cambodia, where the country people slaughtered millions of city people, for no other reason than they were city people. Racism has nothing to do with race or 'blood.' It has everything to do with perception and that perception may take the most ridiculous forms: your faith or race or tribe or nation or class or...The Chief only knows...labels you non-human and thus designated for destruction."

"But hasn't that tendency always been present?" I felt it a most legitimate question and Stopheles recognized it as such.

"Oh, yes! But today we grasp the lynchpin, that any group can be turned against any other group in the most murderous ways, if, *if, If* you can convince them that the opposing group is a species of little or no worth. The Nazis and Communists were both socialists and murdered one another by the hundreds of thousands. Get Republicans and Democrats, Laborites and Conservatives, Christian Democrats and Socialists to demonize one another and then, *bingo,* someday. Downs-Syndrome children – not *really* human – abort! Christians are stupid and the source of all the evil in the world: kill them! Americans are the cause of the world's problems. Nuke 'em!" Stopheles had waxed warm with the concept and now turned hot. "Exterminate them!"

I examined a few more portraits, then noticed that they were hinged. I touched one and the portrait sprang up, revealing a small locked drawer behind it. I looked at Stopheles.

"Ashes to ashes, dust to dust."

"What?"

"This whole hall of a columbarium, filled with the ashes and dust of every murderous petite chief in history." Stopheles touched the Hitler portrait which likewise swung up: "Here we have not only Adolf, but

Eva, even Goebbels and his entire family, all gathered from outside the Chancery in Berlin. Quite an unusual haul, if I do say so. The Chief composed a little verse in memory of the occasion, quite memorable if I do say so myself! It's one of His best, though you should agree they're *all* excellent."

Stopheles cleared his throat twice and went histrionic: "Salm 1111 – *Before He Bids Us All Good Night!*

> "Death has come in his dress whites,
> smiling his second best smile. He clicks
> his heels with a slight bow to each guest.
> He clucks his tongue twice and eyes
> the women darkly. 'Come, come,' he
> purrs, 'let me kiss at least one hand
> with the cold kiss of aspiration.
> Let me nip at least one perfumed ear.'
>
> "He chats with amiable aimlessness –
> how he's called 'Cat' with his black eyes,
> nose twitching for crumbs, how he can
> crawl the floor nibbling gristle and bone.
> How the Fűhrer is dead, a Lugar –
> a Lugar raised to the roof of his mouth.
> How there was cold laughter in hell
> and wings, their violent applause."

Stopheles unlocked the drawer, drew it out, walked over to a waste container, and dumped the contents into it. He turned, grinned, and quipped: "Into the dustbin of history!"

I stammered, nearly speechless. "Birthday….celebrating….why!?"

"Oh, come now, son. They're just dirt. They weren't human!" Stopheles began to laugh and as his merriment gained momentum, it moved toward uncontrollable. "Same principle! I love it! Think of the possibilities for the future! Muslims aren't human. Primitive peoples aren't! The Amish aren't! Criminals aren't. You can go on and on – the future is rich, RICH in possibilities." Stopheles slapped me on the back and led me from the hall.

The tour was over. I was dismissed and hurried back down to what seemed for the moment the safer environs of Babylonia. I sat in the darkness of the bunker, no longer trying to feel, to think, to....

SHALL NOT WE OURSELVES HAVE TO BECOME GOD? ASKETH THE MADMAN[6]

When I'd come down from the Compound and re-entered the city I felt some small relief, the relief of anonymity, but the session had banished none of the deep seated paranoia prior meetings had planted. I double timed my travel through the streets, until I noticed odd glances from the people I passed. Yes, I was acting suspiciously and once suspicious behavior called attention to itself, I knew it would be only a short time before the authorities arrived to collar and question me as to what my big hurry was about. Time to slow down! I forced myself into a normal pace, thrust my hands in my pockets and kept my eyes on the ground immediately ahead of me. My aim was to blend now, to fade into the gray rabble rambling aimlessly by me, and it appeared to work. My occasional surreptitious glances around soon told me no one was paying any more attention to me.

However, I remained so shaken by my latest meetings with Stopheles that I put into practice all the subterfuges I'd seen Faust use, when he thought he was being followed. It took me dark hours of seemingly aimless wandering through the narrowest back alleys I knew to begin to come obliquely at the bunker. "Ten indirections for every real direction," I whispered often to myself, tired though I was and longing for a safe bolt hole in which to rest. It was nearly dawn when I turned my key and stumbled, footsore and fainting into our bunker. I threw myself on a sofa, breathing heavily, just as I heard Faust enter from his room.

"Oh, oh. Worse than I feared," he spoke almost under his breath. He drew up a chair and sat across from me, waiting for me to say something. When I didn't, he slapped his thighs, rose, went to the hotplate and began to heat some grub. Grub seemed to be his answer for most bad situations. "Must have given you another 'magical mystery tour,' as we call 'em," Faust spoke back over his shoulder as he stirred his saucepan.

"What..?" I lifted my head slightly off the arm of the sofa and looked at him.

"You know: the secret room with the painting that's not a painting, more of a living scene like a digital recording of something that happened a long time ago before there were digital recorders. It's beyond The Chief, or Stopheles, or any of them to grasp what happened in that scene and why they failed. They study it over and over and only get themselves so frustrated and frantic, that they lash out at everyone and everything within reach – right?"

I gave a weak nod from the sofa and whispered, "right and wrong."

"Wrong? How wrong?"

"The magical mystery tour was the visit before this last. Yesterday it was the solemn visit to the Hall of Petite Chiefs."

"That's a tad boring, until Stopheles takes ol' Napoleon's or Stalin's ashes and flushes 'em down the toilet. Must have nearly shocked you out of your skin," Faust chuckled.

"Nothing much here shocks me anymore...," but my voice trailed off, belying that claim.

I'd no energy to say more and when Faust asked, "Grub?" I simply nodded in the affirmative. Faust finished his cooking, handed me a bowl, and ordered, "Eat. Then sleep. You'll feel better when you wake up." I wasn't so sure. I wasn't even sure I'd ever wake up again, but then he came close and murmured his stench into my ear, "After all, you survived."

For once, something Faust said buoyed me. Yes, I'd survived. I closed my eyes and slept a dreamless sleep.

~~~~~

I woke as the day closed and found Faust sitting across from me reading aloud. "Once upon a time, there was a madman." I looked up in surprise; Faust smirked back and continued reading:

> Have you ever heard of the madman who on a bright morning lighted a lantern and ran to the market-place calling out unceasingly: "I seek God! I seek God!" As there were many people standing about who did not believe in God, he caused a great deal of amusement. Why? Is he lost? Said one. Has he strayed away like a child? Said another. Or does he keep Himself hidden? Is he afraid of us? Has he taken a sea voyage? Has he

129

emigrated? – the people cried out laughingly, all in a hubbub….

"You're reading Nietzsche!" I sat up straight, more than mildly surprised. Faust had never evinced much interest in Nietzsche, but perhaps that was just to annoy me, Nietzsche lover that I am.

At my exclamation, Faust had nodded in the affirmative. "That's from chapter 125 of" – I searched my mind for the title – "Chapter 125, 'The Madman,' in Nietzsche's *The Gay Science.*" Yes, I knew my philosopher by heart!

Faust shook his head in mock amazement, grinned and crowed, "Give that man a half smoked stogy!" He picked up his reading where he'd left off:

> "The insane madman jumped into their midst and transfixed them with his glances, 'Where has God gone?' he called out. 'I mean to tell you! We have killed him, you and I! We are all his murderers!'

"Yes!" I shouted, my fist in the air in a power salute. "Yes!" Nietzsche always wound me up like that. But then I corralled my jubilation, for I realized Faust wasn't smiling and I knew what that meant. I braced for the ice water splash of his cynicism. This was always his M.O. Draw me in, then soak me with the coldest put-down at his disposal.

His next words surprised me, though, because, instead of a bitter put-down, he spoke in a matter-of-fact tone laced with an undertow of sour regret: "O, we killed the enemy – and we kill him and kill him and kill him – murder him over and over and as many of his followers as we can lay our hands upon. We turn over the soil of whole nations to make graves for them. Our arms grow weary, palsied from nailing him back on his cross. We spit on him and curse him, mock him and dispatch him back to his grave. We roll all manner of stones and boulders over his entrance, but *he won't stay **dead!*** We turn our backs for a moment and he whispers, 'I'm still here, closer than your very breath.'"[7] I struggled to take in what Faust was saying, suspecting that somewhere in his lament he must be mocking me again as usual, me and my Nietzsche.

Faust smiled pityingly. "Don't misunderstand me. Nietzsche's madman was right about something." Faust placed his right hand over his heart – well, at least where his heart was supposed to be – even as he emphatically thumped my chest with his left index finger. "Did *we* not loosen *this earth* from the sun? Can you otherwise explain the grayness that pervades all our days, the darkness that pursues us always? Doesn't each night come on darker, continually darker? Did you not dash on unceasingly in the past and don't you still do so? Aren't we straying, as through our own self-created infinite nothingness? Can't you feel empty space breathe in upon the back of our necks? Haven't you noticed the chill that permeates even your clothing?" Faust fell silent, breathing hard after his rush of questions.

I couldn't help myself: I shivered, shook as if I had developed a severe fever.

"Didn't I just read you the entire history of the last two hundred and fifty years?" Faust was pointed now with his questions. I tried to shrug noncommittally, but didn't succeed.

Faust had paused for breath, but before he could continue, I blurted, "But the crux of the matter is, since we have killed God, shall we not ourselves have to become God...?" At first Faust seemed surprised, even stunned, at my retort, but then surprised, even shocked me as he bent double with laughter, a wild, belly holding, tear streaming manic laughter.

When he finally regained some semblance of self-control, Faust considered me with a gaze that almost might have been mistaken for pity somewhere else. He spoke slowly and with great emphasis, "There never was a more stupid event – and on account of it, all who are born after us belong to a lower history than any history hitherto."

"*NO!*" I resented in the extreme his talking down to me about Nietzsche. "We were born for a higher history – to grasp our destiny, to chart our way to the stars, take control of our own evolution, to...."

Faust gazed at me as if I was the most babbling soul in Bedlam and simply shook his head, "You poor demented stupid fool. Sounds like you've fallen for everything. That drivel makes no sense at all." He could see me smoldering, about to flare forth, my blood hot with anger, but that very anger left me tongue-tied. "You're a Nietzsche worshipper." Faust spat with distaste on the floor at my feet. It was like he had slapped me across the face, begging for a duel. He smiled, could see he'd landed the equivalent by the sour sneer of my lips. I didn't believe in worshipping at anyone's altar, but if I had to choose – and Faust seemed to be challenging me, demanding I do so – *yes,* I'd stand for Nietzsche!

Before I could, Faust said flatly, "You know there's a real problem with Nietzsche's madman, the one who announces God's death." I sensed a trap being set just beyond my field of vision, but couldn't resist stepping into it to see where Faust was going.

"What problem?" I bit.

"His daddy was mad."

"What?!"

"The madman's daddy – Nietzsche – was mad – went right over the edge and took lots of the world with him over the next one hundred and fifty years."

"Granted: he went mad," I rebutted, "but even a madman sees some things clearly!"

"I grant that." I was surprised to have made my point against Faust's normally oppositional attitude, but I could also see that Faust was buying none of my argument, even though I seemed to have scotched his. "Granted, but the fundamental question really is: *did he and his madman glimpse reality or were they out-of-touch with it?*"

I swooped, sensing victory: "Of course they did! They saw our entire situation ripe and whole – the churches and basilicas like so many tombs and mausoleums...." Even as I asserted it with all my energy, I felt the ground slip from under my feet and I'd that uneasy feeling in the pit of my stomach that my argument was about to slip over the edge into free fall.

"Who was the madman speaking to?" Faust snapped like a trap.

"Why, Christians."

"Wrong *again.* At best, hypocrites; at worst, men and women who couldn't really give a whit for God – just like us!" He gave me pause and in that pause I realized he was correct. Faust launched into the rest of his argument like a prosecuting attorney smelling conviction. "Nietzsche's madman was as blind as Nietzsche himself."

"Blind?" I stumbled at that.

"He couldn't see the light all around him. He walked abroad at the dayspring under the broad morning light of the Daystar and saw nothing but darkness. He walked blindly by his own so-called light and when he shattered that lantern before his listeners in the town square, they were dumbstruck by the image: he was a mirror reflection of themselves!"

I stood flummoxed, unable to retort, my mind racing through Nietzsche's madman parable, trying vainly to discover an error in Faust's interpretation. I could see by Faust's very smugness that he knew he'd checkmated all my arguments. Then he said quietly, "The Chief understands: we see only what we want to see, hear only what we want to, speak in error and foolishness: 'see no evil, hear no evil, speak no evil!' A mad philosophy for a mad world! Worthy of Nietzsche's madman. The Chief scratched a little verse that says it all!

> They thought to think like God,
> as if they could stand godlike
> and omnipotent
> at his own stable door
> and fix him for their study,
>
> or worse, play the divine
> Pathologist, render
> the only finding
> possible: The subject
> died by their hands."

Though I'd risen to my feet at the height of our argument, I sat down with a grunt, my mind spinning out of control, as if Faust had just landed a roundhouse knockout punch to my face. I felt numb and Faust saw it. He simply patted me on the knee, rose, and left the bunker.

~~~~~

After Faust buried my faith in Nietzsche in a pauper's grave, I spent a good deal of time wandering aimlessly, both within my mind and within the city. I felt trapped, lost, a wandering soul without an anchor, washed this way and that on aimless tides. Who could save me from the death of everything I had embraced and lived by? *Who?!* The answer finally came to me many days later, a minute before midnight: *The Chief.*

Yes, The Chief. He was the one that held the answers. He was the one to consult and within me my rage grew to find a way to get back to Him, to unburden myself of all my dilemmas, and to proudly embrace His answers. I would brook no opposition: I would plow through all obstacles. I launched my single minded blitzkrieg the following morning.

FEMMISOGYNY

I regrettably had no battle plan, nor weighed what opposition I might meet. Perhaps "weighed" is not the best word, considering The Colonel might try to block my drive. In my rage to see The Chief, I'd stormed into the Central Compound. The various guards who'd accosted me dared not question my jackal pass. Once I flashed it, their belligerent attitudes vanished, accompanied by a click of their heels, a crisp salute, a wave forward down the next hall to the next door or gate. One or two noted with due respect that I was "early," but none questioned my timing further. The jackal pass had more power than I'd originally given it credit, at least enough to get me all the way to my nemesis. Just short of The Chief's chambers, I collided with that 500 pound, five-foot-two mass of female ire and venom who had blocked my approach to Stopheles before my last bitter meeting with him. I flipped her my coin as if she could do nothing but pass me on.

"Business?" She barked as she caught my pass with remarkable dexterity in her pudgy hand, and flipped my coin back to me with the smoothest of returns.

"To see The Chief on important business!" I snapped.

"Stopheles will return momentarily." She turned back to her desk, as unmoved by my preemptory tone as a ten ton boulder.

"I'm *not* here to see Stopheles!" I leaned over her desk, nearly eyeball-to-eye-ball with her, looking as fierce as a mongoose eying a Queen Cobra, and hissed, "I said *see The Chief* on important business!"

She merely stared back, unmoved, set aside a handful of papers she'd just picked up, and said, "*No one sees The Chief, except through Stopheles:* Chief of Staff before The Chief! *Pull-ease* SIT." She pointed to a single chair across the room. I hesitated to obey and she stood up, "*Honey,* I don't have to call the guards. I'll take you down myself, if you don't SIT!" Though she was several inches shorter than me, I knew she was utterly capable of doing it – and much more. Even as I opened my mouth to argue the point, the cold menace in her eyes led me to snap my jaw shut, turn on my heel, and SIT.

"I will SIT, but I WILL see The Chief," was the best I could retort, my intent and bluster deflated, my drive deflected. She ignored me, sat down, picked up her papers and made a series of blunt notes with slashing strokes.

A moment later, I had gathered my wits and was about to speak again, when I heard the staccato of high heels advancing up the hallway. The door knob turned, my unreceptive receptionist glanced up and snapped to attention faster than fat should allow. In stepped the most striking woman I'd seen anywhere in the city: scarlet dress, scarlet shoes, scarlet lipstick, ruby choker, enough eye shadow to make her eyes EYES, and a cascade of blond hair halfway down her back. She was smooth, well rounded, fully packed, appropriately stunning and I was stunned, opened mouthed, salivating, even as I rose to my feet. She turned and considered me from under her long lashes, then turned back to the receptionist and answered, in an utterly masculine voice, "Of course I'll see him," even though no one had made a comment or asked a question.

"*Stopheles?*" I exhaled.

"Come in. Come in, boy. I've just had the most delightful morning, lecturing the girls down at one of the universities." He tossed me a sheaf of papers, the title page of which read:

GEN STUDS 101: GENDER STUDIES 101
Introduction to Feminist ideology Students will study Beauvoir, Bernard, Brown, Dworkin, Paglia, Spender, and others.[8]

Stopheles gracefully sat down, crossed his long, slender legs in utterly feminine fashion, and blew me a kiss. "Well, whadaya think, *boy*? Do I pass? They don't even see through the drag." In one smooth movement, he slipped off his blond wig and tossed it on his desk, where it lay like a long blond dead ferret. "Love the sexual revolution! One of the best things The Chief dreamed up in the last hundred years. The gender bending. The idiot experimentation. Sexual aberration a civil right! Re-engineering the sexes! Radical Feminism setting men and women at war with one another. Humanity, so called, is going to engineer itself right out of existence one of these days! We've made modesty a symptom of repressed desire, self-control suspect, and virtue a vice. Not bad for a mere generation's work." Stopheles' plucked off his ruby ear rings and tossed them in an empty drawer, where they clattered about like dice before coming to rest.

"You should hear my lecture! I call it my 'Rant in *F* Sharp.' It's a masterpiece worthy of The Chief Himself! Yes and I'm a devil of a good teacher, quick as a cane with the smarting put-down. Come into *my* class clear eyed and clear headed and I'll turn that mind of yours to mush. Call me Professor of All Things Problematic and 'Gender Studies' is about as problematic as it gets! All I need to do to look the part is to give my whiskers a wax job, tuck my tail between my legs, and don my most alluring professorial dress. Then I can waltz into class to declaim in my best falsetto voice." I was still absorbing the shock from his earlier entrance and only realized as I caught my breath that Stopheles was launching into a full-blown presentation.

"*Welcome, little sisters, to the brave new world of Feminist Studies. You stand on the cusp of a personal and professional revolution, a dynamic exploration into what it means to be a True Woman.*

"*We've established through our studies that the mother's the greatest threat to an infant. She's almost always discontented and sexually frigid, has no independent grasp of either the world or the future and compensates for all her frustrations through her children. And those children are economic liabilities. No true man likes to cater to inferiors, hausfraus, weak dependent creatures still children themselves!*

"*Sisters, we should give every little girl electric shocks when she sees a baby, so motherhood becomes anathema.* (They titter over that one, not knowing quite how to respond, shocked but intrigued, ready to hear about the world we're advocating). *My advice, my new sisters, is to short those kids or abort 'em. It's your choice, your right, and to my mind it's no choice at all - simple necessity. Child-raising is a poor, no-pay job. It's the community's responsibility, not yours!*

"*Sisters, we must free you for major, serious, adult commitments, or you'll be the sad victims of bad choices – nobody wives doing dead-end housework, wasted lives of boredom, emptiness, drugs, disease and despair after forty. Marriage is no career for a woman, and definitely no sacrament. It's simple prostitution! Legalized rape!*" Stopheles stopped to catch his breath and chuckled: "Idiotic, contradictory, illogical crap – and they sit there for it. No wonder The Chief selected Eve for His very first target."

"One of them always brings up marriage and I cry, '*Don't ever tell yourself you'd be happy married, little sisters. Say that and we'll know you're mentally ill: poor schizoid, brain-bruised, thing-hungry creatures who'll never know commitment*

137

to an IDEA, never risk exploration and real creativity! And don't tell me you can achieve equality by dabbling in those damn painting classes, those little lecture and discussion groups.

"Then I give them *the fair play, no more double standard,* babble: '*Divorce is the best thing that can happen to a woman. It's her declaration of independence! A true woman should have many lovers, keep a married man or two, just for pets. She should be so good in bed her men will never want to leave. That's why you have to hump 'em and dump 'em. But enough for today. We've made a good start. Tomorrow, lecture 2: Independence Day plus one!" Cosmopolitan* magazine's standard on all the reading lists as is the venerable *Playboy Adviser* and *Playgirl.*" Stopheles flipped me copies from the stack on his desk.

Stopheles had punctuated his lecture with an extended strip-tease and reached the bra and panty phase as he ended his histrionics. I'd become so uncomfortable by the entire scene that, when he kicked off his high heels and grabbed a robe from his coat tree, I gave an almost audible sigh of relief. He smiled broadly in response, wiping off some of his make-up with a tissue: "Just call me the 'Distinguished Professor of Femmisogyny.'"

Stopheles sat still for a moment, considering his desk strewn with feminine accessories, tissues, and make-up. "Colonel!" His sharp bark startled me.

"Yes, Professor," and in she marched, not in her usual blue cotton Mao uniform, but in the scarlet robes of an Oxford don.

"Ah, Colonel, I've been explaining our little scene today, since we took our visitor quite by surprise." Stopheles turned to me with a benign glance: "You see, she's one of our distinguished lecturers. She follows up my introduction with her far more tough-minded manner. We send her in to do what we call 'Fem-indoctrination' or 'consciousness razing' on the tougher groups: you know, the girls who think they know what they want and have gotten their backs up against my little introduction. The Colonel comes in to break 'em down, humiliate 'em, re-educate 'em. The Colonel has her very own razor edge!" Stopheles turned back to her, as she obediently stood before his desk, appearing ever so much like a squat black obese obelisk under her mortarboard, "Colonel, give him the works!"

"Yes Sir!" and with that she spun on me, was in my face, spearing my own consciousness with the thrust of her accusatory finger:

"You spread your legs and beg – yes, *beg* –
for everything you have and more.

"Sisters, you should be ashamed of yourselves!
Tell me, if you were a man, wouldn't you think
twice about changing a world where you have
a nice, warm, soft creature trained to treat you
with tender loving care, to change diapers,
and watch his kid doesn't get creamed by a car.

"Goddess forbid you should *dwindle* to a wife!
A nobody wife with a deadend housework job!
Want to know what the life of a housewife is?
Boredom, emptiness, idleness, disintegration,
drugs, disease – and despair after forty!
Housework destroys the mind, renders you
incapable of prolonged concentration, makes
you dull and dumb. It's only suited
to feeble-minded girls, those passive, weak,
grasping feminine things. Say you're
happily married and we know you're mentally ill:
A true man shouldn't have to spend life
living with inferiors, housekeepers,
dependent creatures who are still children.

"You need to be freed up for major, serious,
adult commitments, or you'll be the sad
victims of your own bad choices.
We should ban marriage as a career for women.
Child-raising's a poor, no-pay, dead end job,
and a mother isn't useful to society.
You don't produce anything durable.
You're a poor little parasite.

Get thee to a workplace, sisters!
Get thee to a workplace!

The Colonel, her face a deep scarlet, had gripped me by the lapels about half-way through her rant, pulled me from my chair, and was now shaking me with an anger that threatened to snap my neck, a fact that brought Stopheles to his feet: "Enough, Colonel, enough! I think you've made your point."

She threw me back into my chair with a "Yes sir. Indeed I have, sir. Thank you, sir." She saluted with a click of her heels, and left, closing the door quietly. Only when she was gone did I sit up straight, rearrange my disheveled clothing, and clear my dry throat.

I could neither force a fake smile nor utter a sound, at a complete loss how to proceed. All I could think of was Stopheles' order two sessions ago: *Get the hell out of here!* After the Colonel's raging rant, I was afraid even a twitch from me now might bring worse down. Of course, it wasn't hard for him to see I was completely quelled.

"Now what appears to be the matter?" Stopheles spoke so quietly, so without rancor, that I felt slightly released to answer him.

Yet, even then, I hesitated for a moment, and took a deep breath before making what I had not intended to be a rather meek request.

"May I see The Chief?"

"Why, yes!" He beamed. My eyes widened and I felt somewhat dizzy. *I can see The Chief. I can*...but Stopheles' open grant of permission was too easy.

"Yes? Now? Please."

"Yes, but not now. Sorry, you can see Him at the upcoming commencement in a few days. He's too busy preparing presently. You understand." I wanted so badly to shout, *no, I don't understand. I need to see Him now!* But I couldn't make my tongue form the words. Stopheles continued: "I think you'll be delighted at seeing Him. After all, you *are* The Chosen One, The Chief's keynoter, the hero of our day. You, sir, will be the object of all our attention." I felt the full undertow in those words, drawing me toward the bonfire of my own vanity, teasing and tempting me to believe again in my utter self-importance. I realized too late Stopheles had set me against myself and I was being once more drawn into his orbit.

By now Stopheles had wiped his make-up away and detached his fake eye lashes. He tossed them on the desk between us and they lay there like dead centipedes. He locked his cold black bottomless eyes on me and with unmistakable hardness, "You *do* understand, don't you." Yes, I did understand, did understand I'd better say I did understand, *or else.*

"Yes, sir, I do understand." I said it without inflection.

"Good!" He barked. "You'll receive your invitation to our little ceremony in a few days. Colonel!" He called.

She waddle-bounced in, "Yes, my Lord."

"Show this good man out, will you? I need to see The Chief."

"Yes, sir!" She glared at me and ordered, "*Come!*"

Slack shouldered and slack-jawed, I followed her, completely overmatched and out-maneuvered. I'd been left with one hollow hope, "commencement," and was uncertain even what we were commencing.

COMMENCEMENT

It wasn't until deep into the afternoon that I noticed someone had slipped a black edged envelope, under my door. I stared at it for several moments, before stooping to pick it up. Its face held only the number of the bunker in red letters. I turned it over to see if the return address was on the back, but – nothing – then held it up to the dim ceiling light in my room, again to no avail. The envelope appeared to be card stock and impervious to light. "OK," I muttered and took out my pen knife, surgically slitting one end while gingerly holding the other end with a tweezers, as if there might be a bio-hazard within like anthrax or ricin.

No anthrax! No ricin. Only a small card sized announcement also edged in black and printed in red script.

> ## Chief's Order
> ### Report to Commencement
> ### Midnight in Two Days
> ### The Grand Coliseum
> ### You must present this card for seating:
> #13 - 56789004

I tossed the card on my table and slumped on the sofa. Commencement? For what? Both Faust and Stopheles had told me that I was going through some sort of process or processing, though my meetings with Stopheles in no way struck me as an educational program or special training. Commencement? After picking the card up several more times and reviewing it, I decided only the first line was of overriding significance: "Chief's Order."

"One never ignores or contradicts an order of The Chief." Faust had emphasized that as Rule #1. So I'd show up and see what was up.

~~~

Even if I was blind, deaf, and dumb, I couldn't have missed the Grand Coliseum. First, the place was immense: far larger than the ancient

Roman stadium of the same name. In fact, the "GC," as it is nicknamed, completely dwarfed any of the world's great sports stadia. The Coliseum's very parade grounds would have encompassed several of the size used for the Nazis' Party gatherings at Nuremburg in the mid-1930s. All I could think, as I surveyed the greatness of the place was, *Adolf, eat your heart out.*

But even more overwhelming than the size of the Coliseum was the gut-shaking thunder of thousands of kettle drums in action. And the closer I got to the location, the more I was temporarily blinded by the hundreds of great gyrating spotlights, but I stumbled on shoulder-to-shoulder with thousands of others headed the same direction. The Coliseum grounds and their supporting compounds were ringed by The Chief's elite Praetorian Guards and at the gates efficient armed clerks briskly moved the invitees through inspection, occasionally singling out an individual for ejection and arrest. These souls were removed so smoothly and rapidly most of the host around me weren't even aware of the disappearances.

I stepped to the head of my line, whipped out my card, watched it scanned and the scanner cock his eyebrows in surprise. He clicked his heels, smartly saluted me, smiling: "Number 13! Impressive, sir. You'll be on the dais with The Chief, the Chief's Chiefs, and their special honorees." He signaled me away from the general flow of souls into the parade grounds and another guard of much higher rank quickly led me through the bowels of the Coliseum to special elevators that shot up and delivered us to a spot just behind the high dais. There I was ushered to the thirteenth seat in the third row behind the rostrum. Before me, rank-on-rank, sat the The Chief's Chiefs, each at attention. I spotted Stopheles at the head of the first row and later Bēel near the end of the second row.

The Coliseum's lights dazzled our eyes for another hour, the kettle drums shaking the ground, yea, the very dais on which we sat and then, at midnight's stroke everything instantly fell silent and dark, except for the last reverberation of the drums which must have washed out over, and must have been audible in, the entire city. The affect on the crowd was stunning: a great moan rose from the thousands below us, rose almost to a point of muted terror, then subsided. One drum began to beat and fifty spots from all directions illuminated the rostrum – and The Chief was there, a far larger figure than I remembered and sporting an amazing rainbow aura. "CHIEF, CHIEF, CHIEF, CHIEF, CHIEF," the chant began and rose to a crescendo: CHIEF, CHIEF! HAIL TO THE CHIEF, HAIL TO THE CHIEF, HAIL TO THE CHIEF!" The Chief raised a hand slightly to acknowledge the chant and then stepped away from the rostrum.

A drab functionary took modest charge of the program and squeaked: "The Chief welcomes you," to scattered applause and cheers. "Let me instruct each of you that will cross this stage as to the nature of our ceremony:

> You will lay your flayed skin down if you like
> but hold on to your tongue. Taste how
> bitter it is. Don't empty your pockets.
> Keep your coin, good ballast against rising.

Many in the crowd laughed at this and I could see tiny flashes from several sections of the audience as individuals threw handfuls of coins into the air.

> You can't give us what we already own:
> not your eyes nor your last breath,
> that rank exhalation. Your last green
> sprig of hope maybe? Just drop it
> in the brazier there. Makes a brief,
> but beautiful flare, doesn't it? –
> a rainbow burst fading to ashes and black.
> And that pleasant little dissonant shriek.
> The shock's a bit of a thrill!

Though I winced at the sound, many in the crowd squealed and echoed the shriek as a mocking chorus.

> There now: you'll be free! Forever free.
> Your declaration of independence
> from someone you never liked much,
> the someone you always ignored,
> you know: The Tiresome One
> you'll never hear mentioned again!

At this announcement, the entire Coliseum erupted with wild acclaim and earth-shaking applause, followed by a general CHIEF, CHIEF, CHIEF, CHIEF chant.

The functionary paused and gave the crowd head for its celebration, until I saw Stopheles stand tall and straight, the lights exploring his golden robes. Then, as the lights on the rostrum went out, our emcee announced: "Under-Chief of Chieftains Stopheles will now address you. His subject will be: *Lucifer Loves You – This You Know!*" I did not hear so much as a suppressed cough as Stopheles strolled, all light and fire, to the podium and rested his hands on its polished surface.

> Let ol' Stopheles explain it to you this way:
> every manjack of you thinks you're a Samson –
> all jawbone and long hair, but with the brains
> of an imbecile drooling on Deliah's breast.

Though his opening struck me as an obvious insult, his audience received it with raucous laughter.

> You can't keep your pants up anymore
> than she can keep her dress down,
> but The Chief loves you for that.

More laughter!

> Did I surprise you, saying "He loves you"?
> Well, then, let me count the ways:
> He's the lover of every man and beast,
> Sodom and Gomorrah's most passionate,
> the pimp of all prostitutes who made them
> both male and female. Yes, and He even
> suffers the little children to come on to Him.
>
> Look now! You have heard of our enemy's
> extraordinary love. Why, it is so extraordinary
> that it even comforts Our Chief.

This elicited scattered catcalls, whistles, and general laughter, even as I puzzled what the general joke was.

> You see you want love to be easy – not what
> our enemy showed you, not how hard it could be –
> so Our Chief has good reason to be comforted:
> none of you acknowledged our enemy's love,
> and, better yet, none of you embraced it.

As Stopheles turned back to his seat, the vast throng rocked the Coliseum again with its chant: "CHIEF, CHIEF, CHIEF, CHIEF....." which now ran long enough that most of us were partially deafened by it.

The functionary finally took charge again, having to raise his hands several times, bang his huge gavel repeatedly, and shout into his mike, before the crescendo died. "Now," he shouted, "what you've all been waiting for so long: your very own welcome from Our Chief." The chant began again, but as The Chief stepped forward, He gave a maestro's most magnificent flourish which cut the thunder in mid-chant.

> Yes, now, that's enough my children.
> Quite enough! Welcome to my world!

The Chief stretched his arms out as if to embrace the very universe.

> Yes, this *is* my world and you're welcome to it.

Unlike the crowd's raw humor and rampant jubilation that greeted prior speakers, the response now was utterly focused, respectful, and disciplined. Every soul stood at attention.

> Here everything can be justified if
> you think hard enough about it.
> Must I recite again our mantra
> that evil is good and good evil?

A unified 'NO!' shook the Coliseum.

> No. Of course not. Not on your life!

> This is *my* world and welcome to it.
> You don't have to be horrified when a sniper
> scopes at the babe in its mother's arms
> and delights in the look on her face
> when that tiny head explodes!
> You see, up to now you haven't known
> the worry and pain he's just lifted from her,
> her son's long rejection, her daughter's bitter words
> thrown in her face like so much offal.
> Hear the matricide out about the mother
> she murdered. She might have had good reasons!

Such a bold claim stole my breath, but I caught, to my surprise, a scattering of 'ayes' and 'yeas' from the crowd below.

> Yes, our enemy "loves you," so they say,
> but I love you too, like the pedophile,
> like the pedophile loves his little children.

Again, the Coliseum rocked with the thunderous frenzied chant of CHIEF, CHIEF, CHIEF that this time didn't start of die down until the throng was hoarse from shouting.

When the din died and I looked again at the rostrum, The Chief had disappeared and Stopheles, wearing his most serious demeanor, cleared his throat, his voice hoarse, too, from both emotion and the chanting. A hush settled over the thousands below him and he let the silence grow until even breathing appeared to have ceased. Then, and only then, did he speak, starting quietly and building through the moments toward a climax. "Let us not forget our beginning, how The Chief risked everything for everything, reached for the vast glittering orb of the universe and almost grasped it whole. Let us not forget that even as He closed His fingers on what was His, it was *stolen* from Him – it and every solid thing around Him. The celestial floor on which He stood was yanked from beneath His feet and He heard His jealous arch-rival, Michael, shout, 'Going down!'"

"Was our Chief surprised?"

"NO!" came the unified shout from the thousands below us. "NO!" Even the dais shook with the thunder of that denial.

"No," Stopheles answered quietly. "No and again no, that is our answer! NO will *always* be our answer. NO, Our Chief was not surprised. He knew overreaching came with the grand reward or the grand slip and fall, but it was His confidence game. He was prepared for triumph – *or consequences*. And so Our Chief fell: fell beyond recollection, beyond hope, beyond the last minute modicum of love. How does He describe it in His beloved little volume of *Satanic Sorrows?*

> "I knew it was an exit with no entry,
> so when I fell from that high platform,
> I tucked tight. Sometimes I simply
> cart-wheeled through the unrelieved dark:
> Sometimes I spread-eagled like a sky-diver
> and heard my huge wings flail and riffle
> like half-opened parachutes.
> But mostly I cursed like a pilot
> going in nose first, my curses lost,
> and more than lost in the enemy's silence."

From below us, the very earth seemed to groan and it was a second before I realized that groan actually came from the awed and terrified multitudes below me.

Stopheles, after a pregnant pause to let that wave of terror pass, continued: "Billons of years of falling: an all but infinite fall. Let no one fool you! The Chief knew it is better to reign in heaven than rule in Hell, but He was given only one option: to establish here what He wanted to establish there. That's why He's never satisfied with the here and now and rages against the detritus of existence."

Stopheles took a long breath: "I and a handful of His other lieutenants, this band of renegade brothers," he turned to that first row of dignitaries with a sweep of hand, "we who followed Him down, remember every scene and word of His first commencement in the tiny settlement our Babylonia was then. Yes. We have retained every word of it and let me tell you, it's the law here. Every inductee memorizes it and woe to any sorry soul if he forgets.

"The Chief stood there before us that night, a flicker of His former radiance, a fading light, His great tattered wings flared and fanned huge behind Him, like a glowering backdrop of embers which glowed and subsided, glowed and subsided. He spoke so quietly at first that all of us had to crane and strain to catch the words – but only the first ones! By the last, The Chief was shouting thunder and those words became the great declaration we repeat tonight and to which we pledge ourselves and souls."

Stopheles turned from the rostrum and lifted his arm in a salute. As I glanced over my shoulder, I realized The Chief was glowering from His high throne behind us, glowering like a great scarlet flare. "Repeat after me!" Stopheles ordered:

> "We celebrate You and sing unto You
> for what You believe we shall believe
> for every atom belonging to us
> now belongs to You. You take Your
> kingdoms by subversion and crown
> Yourself with pride.
>
> "Our purpose holds to weary out mercy,
> subvert whatever of nature is contrary
> to You, outlive love, for you are
> impatient and cruel, jealous and
> boastful, arrogant and rude.
>
> "As we luxuriate in Your evil, so do
> we conceive it in everyone's thoughts.
> If we're betrayed, we will not bear it,
> for we are resentment's hot ground,
> the very scarlet spring of vengeance.
>
> "You will demand of us Your own way
> and rejoice in no one but Yourself.

> Here all must worship You or suffer
> the consequences and they are more
> severe than anything we can imagine.

Great silence reigned after the last syllables on those millions of tongues died away. Stopheles bowed deeply to The Chief as did we all and remained with our heads bowed for some moments. Stopheles cleared his throat, turned to the crowd, and whispered, "Thank you," at which point we knew it was safe to look up. We squared our shoulders and I took the opportunity to glance back over my own shoulder to catch one last glimpse of The Chief. To my great disappointment, I found He'd vanished taking his high throne with Him.

At the rostrum stood the drab functionary once more, now introducing the rest of the program. "Some of you have been here a long time, a very long time, and all of you have been here long enough for a commencement. We will be recognizing some for extraordinary accomplishments, others for heroic resistance to the enemy, and still others for," he paused with a grimace, "well, let me put it this way: *your work will be recognized for what it is.*" The last part of his statement carried enough bitterness and resentment to frost the Coliseum.

"We will first single out and dispose of those whose service was 'unmeritorious,' those who have done absolutely nothing significant and thus deserve only a *Dishonorable Discharge.*" I was startled by a searing howl – what sounded like a horrified *noooo* – that rose from far back in the crowd, but, as if on signal, the majority of those near the dais began a loud covering chant of *Yes, yes, yes* and of course, *Chief, Chief, Chief.* From my vantage point high above the arena, I could see several companies of troops rushing to the rear of the throng. The crowd there disintegrated and dispersed in panic under the well coordinated charge of baton swinging troops.

To cover the action and its shouts and screams, our dutiful functionary smoothly jacked up the sound system and addressed the ranks before him. "WHAT MAKES ONE 'UNMERITORIOUS?!'" He boomed. "WHAT EARNS A DISHONORABLE DISCHARGE!?" The amplification drowned out any dissonance, either near us or from the rear, and focused our attention. "YOU ARE THE SLUM-SLUGARDS, SNAILS. YOU ARE NOTHING AND TO NOTHING YOU SHALL

BE CONSIGNED. YOU ARE SIMPLY NON-ENTITIES, NEITHER EVIL NOR GOOD, CRETINS WHO NEVER TOOK A STAND. YOU MADE NO CHOICES, WORKED NO DARK DESIGNS, WERE NOTED NEITHER FOR COWARDNESS NOR BRAVERY, HATE NOR LOVE. YOU PROVED YOURSELF AS WORTHLESS TO THE ENEMY AS YOU HAVE BEEN TO THE CHIEF – WE HAVE ONLY ONE FINAL USE FOR YOU: SPORT AND AMUSEMENT. PRAETORIANS, REMOVE THEM NOW!"

In the ensuing silence, we could only hear the functionary's heavy breathing, before he returned the amplification to normal. One of The Chief's lieutenants in the row ahead of me turned to us and snarled, "Far, far too many of them these days! These commencements just aren't what they used to be a century ago. Where are our Giants? The Stalins, the Hitlers, the Maos?! Where are the death camps and the Gulags?! In those days, The Chief Himself was handing out kudos right and left. We celebrated by wearing swastikas, giving one another Nazi salutes, and dancing the night away to the *Communist Internationale*."

His partner nodded emphatic agreement, put two fingers under his nose and saluted him loudly with a *Seig Heil!* The first ignored him and ranted on, "Nobody measures up today. I tell you, we live in utterly uninteresting times." He grimaced and turned back forward.

Another of The Chief's key lieutenants had heard enough and turned angrily to the first speaker. "This kind of talk is *completely* unacceptable at a Commencement. Yes, we had giants in those times, but your criticism insults Our Chief, denigrating His wisdom, and denouncing His new strategies." The first speaker turned wide-eyed with shock – and fear? The second ignored that surprised response, "The Chief's more subtle approaches today are producing impressive results, impressive in the extreme, *as impressive as in those times, if not more!*"

"No way!" The first stood bolt upright, his face white with rage, and barked, "No way!" The *crack* that followed and that sounded ever so much like a gunshot was from the functionary's heavy gavel, but it quelled nothing and only called further attention to the argument.

"LOOK!" The second roared, his face dark with wrath: "War's good, but sloppy, sporadic, damned well inefficient. Our Chief is far more subtle these days. He uses the law now! Man, consider what He's achieved! Fifty million aborted babies in the United States, 9 out of every

151

10 babies aborted in India are girls! And everywhere whole cadres of men and women chanting 'My Rights! My Life! I'm Entitled!' Millions and millions all legally put away with the approval of the law and better yet by hosts of the enemies' so-call people! And wait until The Chief's new initiatives succeed: the Right to Die movement, government death panels, assisted suicide, every doctor an angel of death.... You've got no imagination!" Other lieutenants gathered around the two just before they came to blows, pulled them apart, and sat them down. The officer at the rostrum, thoroughly annoyed, but also thoroughly flustered, could only watch the action, cowed by their rank from doing or saying anything more.

As the action at the back of the Coliseum crowd and the show on the dais waned, our official emcee smoothly picked up where he'd left off as if nothing had happened. "*Then* we will turn to a category we call 'Studies Extraordinaire,' projects and experiments that have contributed handsomely to our labors, and we will last recognize those of first rank, the rank of *summa cum laude*."

Even though I was supposed to be one of the key speakers and celebrants, I was becoming dozy as the program dragged on. *Interminable* was the word to describe it. Babylonia's everyday mugginess had been enhanced by the body heat and exhalations of so many tens, perhaps hundreds, of thousands confined in the Coliseum and its environs. Our commencement, like nearly every commencement that has ever occurred, was dragging on far too long, speaker after speaker droning on concerning The Chief's accomplishments, His great plans for the future, and His new crop of devotees. My back ached from sitting at attention too long, and my legs began quiver with fatigue, but my spirits rose when we had finally reached the designated highlight of the program, the *Summa Cum Lauds*. That was *me!* Well, correction, that was *us*. There were fifteen of us. Yes, my spirits rose momentarily, only to plummet once more as I glanced down the row of the twelve ahead of me. Them with their official demeanors, their air of self-importance, their stiff, cold acknowledgement of one another. I inwardly groaned, recognizing my torture was nowhere near over. It was obvious that all of us were already bored and none of us really wanted to hear of one another's exploits. We wanted to get our hands on the podium. We wanted the mike. We wanted the eyes of all present fixed upon us, their ears afire with our words, their minds captivated by our vision.

From time to time, I'd caught my companions eying one another – yes, and me - with unalloyed disdain and distaste. We were all in this together, but we were also clearly in a deadly competition for The Chief's attention and favor. I chewed my lip, as I realized that there were no friends among us, no comrades dedicated to a cause, no patriots ready to rally to one another's support and aid.

Our functionary had grown so hoarse that he had to be replaced by a fresh one, who pranced to the Rostrum and announced with lilting voice that it was time to entertain The Chief's most recent discoveries. The applause, scattered as it was tepid, left me crestfallen. I began to feel that we might be a program afterthought, rather than its focus. I shook off that idea with difficulty and psyched myself up for my own personal moment at the podium, vowing that I would re-awaken and re-energize the crowd, whip them into a fresh frenzy, and bring them to their feet, in adulation of me – me and The Chief. The Chief, of course. I would never forget The Chief.

THE 13th DRONE

"Hell is very likely to be modernization infinitely extended."
-Tom Stoppard, *The Invention of Love*

My turn came twelve unexceptional drones later.

The first lectured the crowds into somnolence, the second sealed their eyes, the third sang them a fortuitously brief lullaby, and the fifth rocked them to a deep slumber. As they mumbled on about such obtuse ideas as *The Creative Use of Tribal Genocide as a Population Control Measure; Characterizing the enemy's People as Bigots;* and, the real yawner, *Post-Modernism and Deconstructionism as the Wrecking-Balls of Civilizations and Community,* I dozed fitfully, one ear fixed vaguely on the rise and fall of each speaker's voice, the other quite numb. However, half way through the 10th presentation – a particularly dreary one on *The Universal Movement to Destroy Marriage and Family* – I shook myself awake and began to prime myself for "going on." Yet, my preparation, even then, seemed premature for the next two speakers ran an hour and a half on *Famine as a Form of Agrarian Control* and *Choice: Beyond a Right, a Responsibility of Every Woman!*

When my turn finally came, with the announcement of my topic – *The Sacred Individual Worships at the Inner Sanctuary of Himself* – I found I could only rise slowly and carefully, stretching my tight and tired muscles. The best I could do was wobble to the podium, my legs so stiff, I could barely move them, and certainly with no grace or precision. I felt very much like I did when Faust found me and put me back on my feet. Those feet were as dead now as they were that dark gray day. As I tottered past The Chief's Chiefs, I could see looks of concern on some of their faces, a cocked eye brow here, a shaking head there.

Will power brought me to the podium and, once there, I locked my hands on it, grateful to grip its solidity and steadiness. I swayed with a touch of vertigo, but then focused all my energy on the crowd before me. Only it wasn't there! It had dispersed. Only scattered groups and clusters of picnickers, small gatherings of lingerers and stragglers now remained, concentrating on their own bread and circuses. The ground before the dais had been churned into mire, the air rising from it saturated with the odors of urine, feces, vomit, the pungency of stale perspiration. The vast crowd of hours ago had thinned and those nearest the dais reminded me of those mindless crowds at rock concerts in the 1960s and 1970s, sex in the mosh pits, air rank with the odor of drugs, slurred chatter, and soulless laughter. Several couples danced naked to their own inaudible rhythms. Hundreds of others wandered aimlessly in search of nothing in particular. Many who starred up at me had that vacuous gaze of the utterly stoned, in no state to either see or comprehend.

Our emcee, perhaps seeing my dismay, laid his hand on my shoulder and whispered, "Obviously you've got your work cut out for you. Bring them back to life. Stopheles knows you can do it." He stepped away and I did feel slightly reassured by his comments. To keep the bear of creeping despair from my door, I further bolstered myself by muttering under my breath: *You can do it if anybody can. Watch out world: here I come!* And feeling a tad like The Chief when He made His grab for it all, I launched myself -

"A wise man once said, 'man is the measure of all things'" – and instantly received the strangest feedback from the audio-system *"An idiot once said, 'which man is the measure of all things?'"* I tapped the mike with my knuckle and it crackled and complained.

"You are all individuals. Each of you is number one. Bow to no one."

You are all one with one master. Each of you is number two. Bow only to The Chief.

"You need no one, but yourself. Boldly go where no one has gone before."

You need The Chief. You have no Self. Coldly go where all have gone before you.

Frustrated and appalled, I slapped the mike, but only succeeded in creating a reverberating 'boom.' I glanced at the emcee, who only shrugged his shoulders and gave me a thumbs up. I eyed The Chiefs and noticed their amusement, their smirks, their surreptitious behind-the-hand commentary.

"Damn it!" I cursed.

Yes, damn it, damn it all the system spat. Those still in the arena took up the rhythm, chanting: *Damn it. Damn it all. Damn it. Damn it all. Damn it,* only to have their slogan cut silent by a shriek from the sound system. I smiled to myself. I'd given the mike a harsh twist, which gave me a modicum of silence. I stiffened, stepped back from the podium a minute, considered my situation, and then did the only thing I could do: launched forward with more vigor to push pass the auditory impediment.

"WHEN THE GOING GETS TOUGH THE TOUGH GET GOING!" I shouted.

"WHEN THE GOING GETS TOUGH THE TOUGH GET GOING!" Aha! I congratulated myself. The system had only needed a throttling.

"WHEN THINGS GET HARD, PUSH ON ALL THE HARDER!"

"WHEN THINGS GET HARD, PUSH ON ALL THE HARDER!" Yes! Now I had it and I could see many turning toward the dais, beginning to consider what was being said. Yes!

"I want each of us to realize, fully realize ourselves! Reinvent yourself each day. Make of yourself a thousand new you's. You are the only one who counts – the sacred individual who worships at his own inner sanctuary to himself. Set the crown upon your own head. Be the captain of your fate. Stake your claim to your own soul. You are the most important person in the history of the world. You are the maker of history, discoverer of new universes, inventor of new gods! You, *you*, must become a God among gods."

I smiled to myself. Having gotten through several sentences, I was beginning to find my pace, reach my stride, and the sound system must have been carrying everything straight out as I spoke it, because I heard none of the earlier delayed and garbled feedback. Now they'd really see what I could do!

As I squared my shoulders and cleared my throat to continue, the system cracked like a Howitzer or a jet breaking the sound barrier, the shock of which made even the august members of the party on the dais jump. In the ensuing silence, I heard a *click-click-click,* and, to my horror, I heard my voice uttering utter nonsense: *I want every one of us to realize, fully realize The Chief within us. Vent yourself every day. Take a thousand of you cells new boo. The Chief is the only one who counts – worship Him. Be His sanctuary to Himself. He has the crown upon His head. He is the captain of your fate. Stake your claim with Him. He is the most important figure in the history of the world, the maker of history, claimant to all universes, inventor of gods! And He is the God of Gods, the Greatest God among all gods.*

I'd stopped speaking, but the feedback continued, *You are the onniver of verses, the taker-faker of histories, the inventor of new dogs! You, you are a Dog among dogs.* What remained of the crowd was in stitches, dancing and hooting at the nonsense, and I knew that there was no reason to continue. I gazed across the arena, completely exhausted and humiliated, and stepped down. No one gazed up at me or applauded. They seemed thoroughly unaware of what had happened. I turned and discovered the entire row of The Chief's lieutenants had quietly exited the dais and the two remaining drones waiting to speak, had fallen asleep. Completely deflated, I turned back to the mike one last time.

"Thank you all," I whispered.

Spank you Saul, the system sizzled back. A crescendo of hoots and laughter greeted that and I left the podium demoralized, unable to speak one word more. Scattered applause, obvious in its insincerity, added to my discomfiture. I don't even remember leaving the dais with the rest of the drones, nor how we were all shuttled back to the compound and Stopheles' chambers.

THE RUNNING OF THE JACKALS

*"You're here for a reason, probably a lot of reasons, but like most men and women
in prison, you still claim you're innocent. Get real!"*

Stopheles had required that we "chosen ones" reassemble in his chambers for what he called the traditional after-commencement celebration. None of us was in a festive mood, each of us having experienced complete humiliation at the podium, but Stopheles, himself, was in particularly good spirits, perhaps had imbibed too many spirits, or was high on something else. He opened his liquor cabinet with a sophisticated flourish, surveyed the group of us, and inquired: "Drink?"

All except me readily answered in the affirmative. Stopheles smiled, but then as he caught me with his eyes, I saw them narrow and harden. I squeaked, "No thanks."

"You sure?" He frowned

"Yes."

"Now, you're not off the sauce, are you? Or you just don't like my tastes?" I sensed that I'd be less than wise to answer either of these questions directly, so I simply demurred with the 'bad stomach' excuse.

"Suit yourself," Stopheles, obviously displeased with me, turned his back and poured the drinks, had an aide distribute them. He poured himself a brimming beaker and tossed it down, then observed, "Our real entertainment will be on the great parade ground, not here. We have something traditional in store, our time honored running of the jackals."

"Running of the *what*?" One of the thinnest of our chosen number croaked.

Stopheles looked a tad annoyed, and answered with the sarcasm I had come to expect from him: "Jackals. We're going to run them: you know, *jackals*? The doglike African creature? The carrion feeder? Or perhaps you mistook my reference for the lackey who performs menial tasks, *base ones* mind you, for another? I guess that might be an understandable mistake."

The rest of us laughed knowingly, though we knew nothing. We were as mystified by Stopheles' reference as our tall thin fool was. It was just that he was the first to speak and we read by Stopheles' reaction that we'd better appear to be in the know. Our fool simply colored deep scarlet and faded to the rear of the group, to be inconspicuous. We deemed that move came too late: he'd clearly marked himself.

Then Stopheles focused on me, "Ah, yes, and *you're* here for *more* than the festivities, am I right? And you're here to...?"

Now it was my turn to color, but I could see no way to escape the question and no reason to prevaricate. "Yes, sir. See The Chief and only The Chief."

"Even though you just saw Him at the commencement?"

"Yes, sir. I need to confer with Him in private." I caught the group's barely audible gasp at my boldness – or my stupidity.

Stopheles turned to the group and expansively sighed, "*to confer with Him in private!* Notice," he held up his finger to the group, "I do not even ask about *what*. We expected him to demand to 'see The Chief and only The Chief.' That's pretty common at this point for some of the Chosen."

"At this point?" Always that disturbing feeling that I was a part of something no one had explained to me.

"This point in the process," Stopheles poured himself another drink.

"The process?"

"The intake process, dear boy. Don't you understand? You're being *taken in.*"

"Taken in," I said largely to myself.

"Yes, taken in. Becoming one of us. You're well along in the process and are about ready for the initiation."

"But- but- but-," I stammered.

"But what, boy!? Spit it out!" I was no longer annoying Stopheles; I'd angered him.

"But I thought the commencement was the initiation?" I pleaded.

"Hmmmm," Stopheles seemed to relent. "Some might think that. Yes, I can see that, *but it's not.* You need to realize it's a whole new world and life here and it takes some getting used to. We like to ease you into things, so you're not overwhelmed."

"That's good. I'm feeling that way now – *overwhelmed!* Confused, beset, unclear, depressed, lost."

"Faust can have that effect on some."

I was shocked to hear Stopheles use the name and blurted, "Faust has no love or appreciation of The Chief."

"Probably not," Stopheles' matter-of-fact response just puzzled me more.

"The Chief doesn't care?"

"The Chief doesn't have to care. He doesn't expect to be loved or appreciated – simply obeyed. And Faust is, among many other things, *always obedient*. He helps get folks ready for The Chief's celebrations."

"Or so you think!"

"And so we *know*." Stopheles uttered those four words with such quiet firmness that we all understood he was closing the subject. No more. Nada, if we knew what's good for us. As I glanced at our group, I could see the look of horror on their faces. They were convinced I'd crossed some invisible line and grave consequences awaited me. However, apparently those consequences weren't imminent, for Stopheles turned away and ignored me for the rest of the festivities.

"Come, my chosen ones, let's delay no longer!" He led us forth from his chambers and palace, to a special enclosed viewing stand on the parade ground. Some sipped their drinks, a few like the tall thin fool and I kept well away from Stopheles' view, and hopefully out of his attention. Out on the parade ground, the guards herded hundreds to souls and made them squat before a high dais. One of our group handed me a binocular to get a closer look. On the dais stood another colorless functionary and someone who was dressed very much like The Chief had been dressed when I met him, but…. But I was positive I was seeing a look-a-like, a stand-in, not The Chief himself. In fact, having seen The Chief in all His gigantic, overbearing, terrible ominousness at the commencement, I was now convinced that whoever I'd met when I arrived in Babylonia was simply a stand-in (but no body-double!), a minor counterfeit, at worst, a fraud. Either that – or The Chief was a marvelous shape-shifter. I handed the binocular to the tall thin fool, the only soul I was willing to half-way trust here.

"The Chief?" I nodded toward the dais. Tall thin looked long and hard, several times taking the glasses from his eyes, then raising them again, hoping to focus in better. Finally, he handed the glasses back to me and simply shook his head in the negative, and let his lips mouth the words: "I think not."

The speakers within our viewing stand crackled on and we heard the droll tone of the functionary's voice explaining the sport to those hundreds of souls who were about to participate. "Here's how our little game goes: There'll be multitudes like you, all quite suitably and similarly prepared. No one will speak, but The Chief," the functionary motioned and bowed to the stand-in on the dais, "because He loves this moment, its mock drama. When He briefly stops smoking and draws a long breath as if savoring His aromatic tobacco – something between honeysuckle and yew - He'll close His book, tap His pipe on the edge of His ash tray and smile. He'll say, *'ashes to ashes, dust…but enough! Let me tell you a story.*"

"Some can whimper if you like, or smile back weakly, or be sick, if you feel the need, as many of you will. You can shuffle and cough and study your shoes, if you like. *However,* none of you will touch, consider, or embrace one another. You'll not sit down or make yourselves comfortable, because you're supposed to be most uncomfortable. The Chief will consider his long fingers, their black nails. Then as all of you, even the best among you, grow extremely uneasy, He'll open His little book of *Satanic Salms and Parables*, and give you a reading.

The ceremony, indeed, went as outlined and when the time came, The Chief calmly rose, took the microphone, and intoned the tale. Yes, it was His voice, the same suave, precise, cultured voice I knew from my meeting with Him.

> *"Upon a time very much like this,*
> *there lurked beasts hereabouts,*
> *very close to us here, yes! Beasts*
> *as relentless as sin, as evil,*
> *locked too long in hell and not*
> *allowed to run wild abroad*
> *over the earth. They growl*
> *no end to temptations. They whine*
> *and hunger and thirst and are never*
> *satisfied. They draw the quick breath*
> *of impatience, hot with rage*
> *at old slights, all their hoarse*
> *and violent throats baying for blood.*

161

Here The Chief paused, surveyed the crowd, and leaned forward as if we fully knew what he was talking about.

> *"Perhaps you've seen them, yes?*
> *Perhaps one evening you've looked back*
> *along your trail and glimpsed their*
> *unmistakable tracks, intermittent,*
> *but desperately persistent – the sign*
> *of the beasts that stalk you down your days?*
> *The occasional glint of reptilian eyes,*
> *dead steady, staring back?*

Here The Chief paused for signs of recognition and there were some: some who whimpered again, others who simply shook their heads *yes* in acknowledgement, and many who simply shook.

"*Welcome, souls, to tonight's sport: The Running of the Jackals!* At this point, The Chief turned, handed His mike to the emcee, and retired to His easy chair.

The emcee launched back into his spiel like a carnival barker: "Who will do the running? You will! You will run for your lives. Where are the jackals? Oh, those big boys are kept in kennels out of sight and big boys they are, ferocious and mean, much larger than most of their species, and rabidly hungry. They'll be running too – *after you!*" Even within our enclosed viewing stand, we could hear the terrified wail of the mob. We watched some break ranks and begin to run. A few fainted and a number of others knelt before the dais begging it was not so. Though the functionary covered the mike with his hand, we could hear his muffled, "Mercy? *Mercy?* Where in the world do you think you are? Mercy's not our stock in trade."

Dozens of souls pressed up to the dais, but it was far too high to mount. They appeared to be begging for direction and direction they got. The functionary barked: "You ask what you should do?! *Run, you idiots!* Run for your sorry souls. Run, for they depend on how fleet of foot and shrewd you are! When The Chief signals RUN, hot foot it out of here."

All of us watched, our eyes large, our hearts pressing our throats, our foreheads dripping perspiration. No matter how tough and unfeeling we were, this scene was difficult to watch. The Chief drew a pistol, one that we thought was a starter's gun, until he pointed it at the crowd and pulled the trigger. One of the foremost in the group dropped, shot in the forehead, and the rest turned and stampeded in terror. Before they'd made the first hundred yards, a dozen poor sots had been trampled to death. As they crowded through the triumphal gate at the parade ground's further end, we could again hear the functionary's matter-of-fact voice:

"'My Lord?'"

"*Yes.*"

"Now what?"

"*Same as always: Give them three minutes head start and then release the beasts.*"

We listened to the functionary tonelessly count down the minutes and seconds, and watched The Chief relight His pipe. In spite of our distance from Him, we could see His tobacco flare scarlet. He waited, waited – one, two, three minutes – and then smiled as another voice cut across the functionary's: "JACKALS AWAY! THE JACKALS *ARE* RUNNING." We watched in horrified silence as the great pack of snarling, rabid beasts broke into view, sprinted across the parade ground in seconds and disappeared through the arch. As the parade ground emptied of any further spectacle, we stumbled from the viewing box. Many of us covered our ears, but to no avail: we could still hear somewhere out of sight, but far too close in earshot, the nightmarish screams and shrieks of the victims.

After we returned to Stopheles' chambers, we fell into an orgy of drinking in an attempt to forget what we'd witnessed. It would be a vain attempt and simply impart the added pain of a major hangover. Someone in his whiskey-soaked fog slurred out the question that most of us had, but only he was stupid enough to ask: "What will you do with those who run fast enough, the survivors?"

Stopheles simply studied his glass for a moment, looked up, and grinned: "*No one can run that fast.* There won't be any." Our drinking continued almost to morning.

THE PYROMANIACS OF HOLOCAUSTS

"You might be wondering – the hard-men among you, the nutters, the glassers, the thugs – whether you couldn't hack it in Hell, whether you couldn't, when it came right down to it, butch the bastard out. Well guess what: You couldn't.
-Glen Duncan, *I, Lucifer*

"I *will* see The Chief." Bold I was and confident, or perhaps stupid and over confident. No more Mr. Nice Guy. No more being put off. No more delays. I deserved more than the treatment they'd given me: that raw humiliation at The Coliseum, that violent atrocity at the Grand Parade Ground. Stopheles soaking us in liquor and our own vomit at his drinking orgies. And always the Colonel blunting my efforts with her super-sized denials and Stopheles diverting me to his own sorry purposes. "*NOW!*" I shouted at The Colonel.

"You will," she replied mildly without even looking up at me.

"*I* will?" I stammered at that response, expecting violent resistance.

"You will," came the same mild reply.

"Now?"

"But first you'll talk with The Chief's number two: my lord Stopheles."

"Now wait a minute!" My hackles went up. The same old run-around! The same old diversions and prevarications, the same old….

A hand gripped my shoulder from behind. I whirled, and found myself in Stopheles' swallow face. Caught off balance both physically and emotionally, I allowed him to guide me into a palatial office. He rounded his ornate desk and settled in his chair, regarding me even more mildly than The Colonel had.

"Now, boy, what's the problem?" Stopheles made the question sound every inch like that of a caring friend, but I wasn't buying it. I'd been here too many times before.

"The problem is: I want to see The Chief **now**!" I could hardly believe I was continuing to carry my demand so forcefully forward.

"That *is* a problem."

"Why!" It was a demand, not a question.

Stopheles answered with continued mildness, "Because He's not available right now." I swelled with scarlet anger at that response and was about to flame forth when Stopheles continued, "*But* you shall see The Chief within the next twenty-four hours."

That didn't mollify me. "Another put-off."

"No."

"See *and talk to*," words from Stopheles could be as slippery and charged as electric eels and I was taking no chances.

"And talk to," his mildness held.

"How do I know you'll keep your promises?" Insulting as it was, I had to ask the question.

"That's *not* my job," Stopheles spoke those last words so quietly I almost missed them, but they began to sink in, "but what I said is no promise, simply *fact*."

That caught me flat, "Fact."

Stopheless still regarded me mildly, in spite of my continuing disrespect, but his diversions and denials, or whatever they were, no longer stoked my fire. It was burning out as quickly as it had flared. At that very moment, Stopheles replied, curtly, but evenly, and with huge condescension. "Now listen to me: I love you and so does The Chief." Stopheles smiled and continued matter-of-factly: "Did I just surprise you, saying that? Yes. Perhaps you weren't listening at the commencement."

Except I had been listening, avidly listening, at the beginning of that interminable program and now those words seared across my mind: *The Chief and I are lovers of every man and beast, Sodom and Gomorrah's most passionate pimps of all prostitutes who made them both male and female. Yes and we even suffer the little children to come on to us.* For the first time, the utter truth of those words bit home and I felt what the rabid dog must feel, completely disoriented and deranged, ready to tear even himself. My throat closed and I couldn't bark, let alone howl. I could only groan something between a gargle and a growl: G-g-g-g-g-o-o-o-o-d...."

"Pull-ease. If anything is taboo here, *that* name is." Stopheles said it so quietly, it didn't seem he was offended. He simply became even more condescending, if that was possible, and apparently it was. I twisted around, stumbled backwards, dizzy with vertigo, tripped against the edge of a leather sofa, and fell into it, helpless and foaming. Stopheles rose from his mahogany desk, came around, drew up a chair, sat, and leaned forward until his face was only a foot from my own. When he spoke, I heard the absolute zero in his voice: "You are a complete disappointment to us, a nothing, never good at anything, not even evil. Don't get me wrong: while you've never been good, your fault is that you've been simply evil by default, a man-child with a simpering brat's attitude and entitlement expectations. No wonder you came here! And we've only one place for the likes of you."

Dazed by his denunciation, I thought Stopheles might soften it in his next breath, but he stood up and laughed coldly at my confusion, turned his back on me and ambled back to his desk. Stopheles grinned across the room at me, now cowering in the corner of the sofa. Then, he waved me off like an annoying mosquito. A moment later the Colonel opened the door to find me retching on the floor in front of the sofa. She was neither surprised nor concerned, but simply stepped around me and saluted Stopheles: "Yes, Prime Minister."

"Put that in a holding cell until he's ready to go to The Chief."

"Yes sir."

"And then come and clean this mess up."

"Yes sir."

"And get his pass from him. He won't need it anymore, since he won't be going anywhere."

"Yes sir." I felt her hard hands grip me around the shoulders and hoist me to my feet. Dazed as I was, I let her drag me out of the door, down the dimly lit hallway to room 557, where she tossed me on the floor inside.

I heard a well-oiled bolt being thrown. Thrown down. Locked in. Imprisoned. A dim bulb glowed fitfully over my head, but cut out every few moments, leaving me in stultifying darkness. If only I could see The Chief...they said I was going to see The Chief, but was that simply playing with the mouse in their paws? If I could only see Him once more, something might be put right. If I could only leave something behind, something that said I was here, something.... I felt for the tiny microprocessor in my waistband. Still there! My recorder, my micro-disks. I *could* leave something behind. I could and I would. I gingerly picked the seam apart, until I could pry out the unit through a slit in the waistband. I spent the next hours in darkness, weeping and whispering the sorry events of the last few days into the record, finally stuffing the unit and disks back into my waistband. Exhausted, I dozed in the dust and woke only to find myself soaked in my own urine. The bulb blazed overhead and Faust grinned down at me.

"You!"

"Just stay down. No need to get to your feet in my honor. You'll soon need all your strength," Faust sounded almost kindly, but I was beyond any further pretense on his part.

"What are you here for?" I coughed in the dust.

"Ah, good! Right down to business now. You've learned something, I see." I resented in the extreme his condescending grin, but was helpless to do anything about it.

I spat through the dust on my lips: "Not something – *everything!*"

"No. Not everything – yet. That's what I'm here for now: to prepare you for your meeting."

For a nano-second, hope flared in my heart – meeting usually meant decision: was it going to be *take it or leave it?* – but one glance at the cruel glint in Faust's eyes told me that leaving was not in the equation and I dreaded to know what I might be offered. *Guillotine or drawing-and-quartering? Brains blown out or bashed in?* NO THANK YOU!

Faust ignored me and began: "We'll head down the road soon. The way's rather steep and slippery, but don't worry: you've already fallen further than you ever thought possible."

"I haven't eaten or drunk anything for hours, maybe days!"

"You can of course ask for a drink, but you'll find the cup brims only with nightshade and the bread here's wormy and mostly wood fiber. Given our meals here and your appetites, you'll dry up like a husk in the last long August heat, but you already know we've got plenty of that kind of *heat.*"

I murmured something as I lay face down on the floor listening to Faust babble on.

"What?" He nudged me face up with his foot.

"I said, *I didn't sign on for any of this!*"

Faust bent double with mean laughter. "Oh! O, now you tell me! You must have come for the *Better Homes and Gardens* tour, right? That don't wash any better than a toad trapped in a cesspit. Remember when I told you, you weren't no Dante and I wasn't no Virgil? Poor simpering fool, you were probably expecting some Beatrice up ahead."

Faust chuckled, as if a fresh thought had just entered his mind: "You know they don't study Dante anymore. Let me recite you one of our Chief's most famous *Salms:*

> You fools mark him down as an early day
> evangelical. You grimace and snigger
> over his hell fire and brimstone clichés,
> that vengeance he dreamed up for each
> of his enemies. Yet, he touched the ice
> at the heart of our world, trod the
> almost impenetrable darkness
> in the depths of the pit. Dante, at least,
> knew who and what he was dealing with.
>
> Yes, ignore me. Look away! Call us
> what you will here. We're still
> the silent partners of all serial killers,
> the *Ubergruppenführer* for all
> concentration camp commandants,
> the Commissar for Liquidations.
> We're the dancers who delight at the sight
> of limbless children, their suppurating
> wounds, those mutilated bodies swelling
> under the African sun. We're the pyromaniacs
> of holocausts, the burnt offerings of which
> I, The Chief, am only too pleased to accept.

I rolled back unto my face, no longer wanting to stare into Faust's broken and cruel visage, but he yanked me upright by the scruff of my neck, unwilling I should ignore him. "You're almost ready to meet The Chief now," he crowed. He shoved me against a wall, began to dust me off, but thought better of it. He simply held me there, his breath nearly anesthetizing me. He looked into my watering eyes, heard my gagging, and let me slide down the wall. As I slumped over on the floor, he was interrupted by a knock at the door. "Yes!"

"You're needed in room 467." The Colonel's voice.

"I'll be back!" He spat at me as she threw the bolt and let him out, but she didn't step back out and lock me down. She walked up, gave me a swift kick with her boot's steel tip, a kick that left me helplessly gasping for air, while she bent over and gave me a thorough frisking.

"Uh huh," she grunted as she fished my micro-disks from my waistband. "As I suspected!" She gloated, carefully dumping the evidence into the breast pocket of her tunic. "A little bed-time listening for the Prime Minister. He needs a good laugh these days." She gave me a second breath-banishing kick, slammed the door behind her, and threw its bolt, leaving me to gasp, writhe, and whimper in the dust.

THE NETHERS:
DARK REGIONS ROAD

You hope to dialogue with the Devil, huh? Bad idea!
Unlike God, Satan doesn't listen to you. His only response is a constant dribble
of babble, largely nonsense, calculated to confuse, seduce, and abandon.
-The Midnight Monologues, *Simon Deadfisher*

So, here I am at what appears to be the bottom of my remembered death and I'm marching with dozens of others to the beat of a different drummer, a ragged beat, down a road I seem vaguely to recall. Perhaps our new two-step came from our drag-and-shuffle gait, as if each of us was dragging a game leg, or was shackled with a heavy leg-iron. Or was it from my extreme fatigue or from the waning of the day's heat? After all, it seemed summer and evening. I considered the dust on my disintegrating shoes, one missing its heel, the other missing its sole. I considered the dust edging the cuffs on my torn trousers, the perspiration soaking my tattered shirt.

And I thought: Where *are* we? How did we get *here*? Where's Babylonia? How in the world will we find our way back? We're not really supposed to be here, not now, *are we*? As we stumbled down a stiff slope toward a greater dark, I recalled occasional snatches and flashes of memory, sharp and cutting as razor edged jigsaw puzzle pieces. A violent drunken binge with Stopheles. Repeated images of Bēel scuttling down one hall after another just ahead of me. Every door he unlocked merely opened on another dim hall and every hall ended before another rusty locked door. Once or twice I muttered to him - "Come on! What's going on here?!" – merely to have him turn and set those bug-eyes on me with a big knowing grin.

Was there deep, dreamless sleep? I'm uncertain.

Had I walked myself to exhaustion on Babylonia's stinking streets, like a lost Alzheimer's patient left with only fragmentary memories? On my rambles, Faust occasionally materialized like a phantasm floating a couple of blocks ahead of me. He never glanced back and always

170

disappeared into an alley's shadow. It happened enough times that I marked it up to my over-worked and exhausted imagination.

Our straggling line-of-march, if I could call it that, stumbled past a road sign and one or two of us looked up to read its inscription: *Dark Regions Road*. I stopped stark in my tracks and stood there staring until one of our wandering hindmost bumped mindlessly into me. I cursed and thrust him aside. He tripped, fell, picked himself up, and staggered on his way head down without so much as a sound.

Dark Regions Road. I'd often walked such a road as a boy with my pals. It had never been paved and ran out of town a few miles to a handful of played-out hill farms. What both intrigued and terrified us as children was the way the road rose and fell over the rolling landscape, descending every so often into a gloomy, tree shrouded dip. When we explored the road near twilight, these regions spooked us and we'd dash breathlessly through them and out into the mellow amber of the evening sun bathing the rise. When night fell, the thought of entering one of these areas absolutely terrified us. The worst of the dips was near the end of the trail as it entered the hill country. Within that darkest of the road's dark regions lay the yawning maul of a great cavern, a cave that grew in my young mind to mythic proportions, an ominous hole, a devouring dark. We always made our most desperate dash past it, screaming up out of the draw as if legions of demons pursued us. Once one of my less watchful companions trod on a yellow jacket ground nest and we fled shrieking in real terror and pain, stung repeatedly.

Now, no longer young, though to my mind, I wasn't old either, though indubitably dead, I seemed to be ambling down into that same region and could feel once more a little twist of that youthful anxiety. Perhaps the highway department had cemented a cap over the cavern's entrance. After all, it had never been safe. As boys, we'd been told stories by our elders, stories of boys that had insisted on ignoring their parents' warnings and decided to explore the cave, stories of the long and unsuccessful searches for them. Once one of my friends pointed to a grave stone in a local cemetery and told me it was for one of the lads — but his body wasn't buried there. Who were we to question such a claim, or worse, seek to find out whether it was true or not the only sure fire way we could think of? *No way*!

Other stories reported that cave seemed to go down forever, spiraling ever deeper into the earth. Some said it held a bottomless pit, others a labyrinth of caverns, each opening to something larger and more ominous. Some locals reported that several spelunkers had disappeared into it over the years and had seemingly been absorbed by the earth or - as other, more optimistic locals had it - emerged hundreds of miles away.

I shook off my memories as I caught sight of another sign, an arrow pointing along our line-of-march. As I neared it, I glimpsed only the name: *Tierra del Fuego.* I continued to put one painful foot in front of the other. *Tierra del Fuego.* That didn't compute. No Spanish names at all in the area in which I grew up. Our present road, which had begun as a narrow path in the scattered outer suburbs of Babylonia, had widened considerably, widened enough to accommodate The Chief's own Boulevard, though now it only held our meager, scattered line of stragglers, and we must have been strung out across the miles. We'd lost at least one of our number, who collapsed and could no longer rise. We marched past, ignoring his prone body, not unable to help, simply unwilling. Many of us made a wide berth of it, passing him on the other side of the road. No Samaritans we!

Dark Regions Road. No. This was not the road of my boyhood. No cavern yawned black and sinister ahead of us. The great waste stretched off around us, though right before us it fell away into one of those desolate craters like the ones that appear in photos sent back from the various Mars Rovers and Explorers. Even from our vantage point on the crater's lip, we could barely spot the other side. We didn't halt to enjoy the view, because there was nothing to enjoy. We simply continued down into the crater as if our bodies were directed by some homing instinct, though none of us felt we were headed home. After reaching the crater's dusty, rock-strewn floor, we found our way almost worthy of the Boulevard back in Babylonia. The surface appeared to be paved with large regular polished cobblestones. Two or three of us knelt and ran our hands over their smooth surfaces, only to wince back. Skulls! Each "stone" was actually the dome of a skull! I stood bolt upright, then staggered sideways, nearly passing out from the quick movement. I steadied myself, gathered my breath, and by a sheer act of will closed my mind to the "cobbles," not willing to consider what they might mean. I shuffle-traipsed my slow way onward and others followed, apparently having thought better of thinking too.

An exhausting day later we crested the opposite rim of the crater through a wide defile and surveyed the way before us – only there was *no way before us*. Our skull paved road ran less than another thousand yards and ended abruptly at the edge of an immense chasm. As we hobbled the distance to the edge, the size of the void appeared to grow. Its vague curvature to the right and to the left of us ran miles before disappearing into the gray opaqueness that hung over the land and passed for atmosphere. Strain as we might to catch sight of the opposite side, we failed. "Must be wider than the English Channel," one of our number with a British accent muttered.

Another of our number startled me by clutching my arm for an instant, pointing to something among the boulders and low dunes near the chasm's edge about a hundred yards ahead. Something small boned, short in stature, appearing to be only a tad larger than a dwarf: It squatted there, staring across the void, with a face that looked ever so much like that of a leper resting in his rags or a large poison toad or a small komodo dragon. Its very appearance would lend a by-passer bypassing quickness to his steps, even though the creature's size and demeanor suggested it was not likely to stop anyone. Our line, though, with obvious repugnance, had begun to make a wide detour away from it in an effort to hurry past, a detour the creature ignored as a sort of counter-snub to those avoiding it.

My problem was: I was no longer watching where I stepped. I stumbled, twisted my ankle, and fell heavily face first on the path's sharp stones and ashes. As I lay there stunned, I heard the gravel crunch as someone approached. "So you've finally arrived," an all-too familiar voice muttered. I spit blood, my throat raw as if I'd swallowed a shot of ground glass and ashes. Face down, I'd breathed volcanic dust, gagged, and raised myself on bruised hands and knees, to see who or what had spoken. It stared down at me with a mischievous glint in its eye as I half-choked out, half hissed: "*Faust!*"

"You seem surprised to see me."

No, I wasn't. I wasn't surprised at all, more like *appalled*. "No. And I won't even ask what you're doing here."

"You don't have to: I'll tell you." And he turned to the whole of our number bunching up as our line slowed and stopped and gathered around the two of us. "I'm your own one-and-only, whole-and-entire welcoming committee." Some watching our exchange turned aside to continue their slow shuffle toward the chasm's lip where they halted and stood like so many damaged manikins or exhausted zombies.

I hadn't moved or risen, but turned back to Faust with renewed fire in spite of my fatigue. "*You, you brought us here.*"

"I did *not.*"

"Then who would you blame?"

He cackled and slapped his knees. "Nobody, boy. Nobody! You don't get sent here. What they say is true: You come bearing the shadow of your former life over your shoulders, having discovered the way all by your perverse self. Yes. You've dragged yourself all the way here, made all the narcissistic demands on others you could possibly make, consigned all your women to serial prostitution, sacrificed your children to Moloch, and transformed your heart into a cold urn to hold their ashes.

"The Chief has a wonderful *Salm,* ol' 666, as we call it here. It's His most remarkably personal *Salm* and it's like you can literally hear Him speaking every word to you. I think it explains your situation perfectly." Faust cleared his throat and intoned with more than a little pompousness:

> "Go ahead. Tell me your life's short story
> again, that boring tale of sordid desires,
> all your mean degraded ambitions.
> How you always wanted to win the lottery
> for all the good it would do.
> I'll lean forward again, rapt with attention,
> my eyes fixed on your babbling lips,
> as you cross and uncross your legs.
>
> "I promise I'll listen with all the intensity
> of a close friend, as I strain to catch
> each faint click of the tumblers, their sequence,
> hidden within or behind your words.
> Then I'll try my own touch and know I've got

174

it when the vault of your heart swings open
and beyond shines your soul's small treasure.

"I'm more subtle than a smash and grabber.
When I lift your life, you won't even feel
me slip away everything that makes it
worth living.

"Later, much later, when you think back over
our conversation, you might realize
whatever you heard from me is not what
you thought I said, but only what you wanted
to hear. Whatever I gave you was not
what you needed, not even what you wanted,
though you thought so at the time. And you will
wonder why you ever thought I'd give you anything,
I who take everything, who leave nothing
behind me."

"Yes. Now welcome, my boy, to The Nethers. A place that is not a place. Minutes without moment. Time frozen in black ice. The Nethers: the long dark of it is impossible to measure. Try as you may, all your calculations end nowhere. Scan the darkness above you? No pole star. No Dippers. No Southern Cross. You don't even have a coin for a boatman – for there's no such creature. You have finally found a point without reference, where money buys nothing and love no longer exists."

As he gushed on with his flow of babble, my head cleared, and – capturing my breath with deepening, but still excruciating swallows – I was finally able to focus on the face leaning down over me. Pocked. Lips chapped. Breath like a..., (I gagged on rising bitters). Nose broken and flattened. One diseased eye, a sightless white, the other.... He grinned. "Ah, now! That's better! Look me in my eye and me tell all the soul and body scars were worth the sufferin' and I'll tell thee as big a lie of mine own making!"

I raised myself on my elbows, bracing myself against the tremors of pain tightening across my back. He made no effort to help. "Who?" I winced out.

"Who, what, where, when, why, how? You're gettin' there, boy!" He gave me a short, sharp kick in the hip.

"OUCH! Damn it! Why…" sitting more fully upright.

"Ah-ho! Ah-ho, a butt to the buns, that always gets 'em moving," he danced shy of my attempt to grab his leg and drag him down, a dance of such deftness it belied his ruined appearance. Before I knew what was happening, he'd danced a half circle around me and gave a second sharp kick to my other hip. "Hopalong Cassidy if I do say so myself," he chortled. He had been about to try the whole move again, but anger laced pain super-charged me to my feet. He danced away, instead, dukes up, like a belligerent leprechaun, menacing for a fight, but it was a mocking bluff. "Hi-de-ho, Joe. Glad to make thy acquaintance!"

"Just who the hell are you anyway?" I hissed. I would have growled, but my seared throat would have none of that.

"Just who the hell does he think he's askin' 'just who the hell are you?'" Dwarf, leprechaun, short stub of a person, Faust, he seemed to be histrionically addressing the air around us. "Well, now, fella, forgotten so soon? I'm only your familiar, remember?"

"And what is *this?*" I gestured toward the yawning chasm, on the edge of which the rest of our group had gathered now. Its immensity dwarfed them to such insignificance, they appeared like microbes on the lip of a huge Petri dish.

"O, come now, pull-ease! You couldn't have forgotten your Dante this quickly! We took down the sign centuries ago, but it's the same old place it always was, even when ol' Alighieri passed this way."

"Hell's mouth?!"

"The very same!"

"But what was back there? What was Babylonia?"

"Just the beginning that leads inevitably here."

"You're a damned liar and a cheat," I growled under my breath, but he heard it.

"Well, thank you. It's what we do." Then, as if that needed any explanation, Faust added: "Everyone lies here. Haven't you noticed?" I plopped back down in the dust, my legs no longer able to support me, then collapsed completely, face first, as if struck dead. "Yep," Faust mocked, "one day you wake up dead. Then ol' Faust has to come out and gather you up. Problem is, once you're awake, there's no real sleeping on The Chief's time."

Faust simply gave me one more swift kick, this to my temple, one that left me writhing in the dust, foaming, as lost for words as a stroke victim struggling to find his vanished language. "Well now, enough of this mindless chit-chat." I shrieked in head and body pain as he yanked me up, threw me over his shoulder, and carried me roughly through the crowd which stumbled backwards to make way for us. They gazed, listless, unfocused, uninterested.

He stood me briefly on the chasm's lip. It fell away below my feet like a sheer continental shelf, and as I wavered there, gazing into the void's depth, Faust whispered in my ear: "Not bottomless, but nearly so." As unsteady as I felt, I tilted my head (Faust having with a firm grip on my collar), for I thought I caught a suspiration, perhaps a minimal whisper from below. In spite of my throbbing contusions, I focused harder and heard more than a whisper. Whispers! Rising and falling hisses of whispers, then murmured words, punctuated by screams and shrieks. Others around the edge of the pit leaned forward as the voices and howls became more distinct. One or two wasted both in body and mind began to freak, drooling, wild-eyed, their movements jerking left and right the more they listened, and then the first just quietly threw himself over the edge, his flailing body disappearing into the void. I snapped upright, nearly knocking Faust backwards, then watched horrified as two or three more fainted and faded over the rim. Faust gave my collar a rough shake and growled, "Watch it, stupid. You'll get there soon enough." A second gibbering idiot pushed aside those around him, shouting wildly, and colliding with yet others, until a whole mass of those thrown together by him tripped like a tipsy knot of drunks and toppled into the blackness taking him with them, a screaming mass of flailing arms and legs that grew smaller and smaller until they faded and vanished.

"No!" I shouted and wrestled against his grip, but couldn't break it, though we stumbled dangerously close to the pit's crumbling lip. I was sure Faust was about to cast me in, when he snarled in my ear: "The Chief sank it especially for folks like you, so you could experience something of what He did. It's His aim to fill it brimful with wilted, desiccated souls like yours, and let me tell you: He's got a long, long way to go yet, but there's plenty like you to supply the filling."

"No!" I screamed as Faust jerked me around, then dragged me back from the abyss and cast me in the dust at his feet. Surprised, I looked up, but he'd already turned and began to step away.

It's "Bye and bad riddance! I'm done here."

"Wait!"

"No. I'm wanted elsewhere."

"What am I – what are we – to do?"

"Figure it out."

"It's going to be dark soon. How are we to find our way back?"

"You're not supposed to, dummy."

"Then what are we to do?"

"Stare into the abyss. Stare into it long enough and you may sense it staring back and when you see it grin wickedly and beckon you'll know – they'll all come to know – what to do.

"Do?" I shivered in the chill night air flowing down around us and into the chasm.

"*You know!* Like the fellow with acrophobia who has an overwhelming urge to jump. Just follow your nature, boy. You always have!" I sat in the dust where Faust had thrown me and listened to the hollow slap of his retreating footsteps as he headed back up the way of skulls. I considered following him, but lay back exhausted, so I crawled nearer the chasm and settled with my back to a boulder, staring into the void, waiting for sleep, sleep that wouldn't come though the impenetrable dark closed in around me until I could see nothing and I could only hear the void's suspiration. Sometimes it sounded like a woman breathing and moaning in her sleep. Sometimes it seemed to whisper sweet nothings. And occasionally, it placed a hand on my thigh and begged for me. And sometime in the night she drew me up and I shed my rags. She took my hands, placed them on her cold breasts, and led me on over the edge.

NETHERWORDS
A Netherlude

What in hell is the Devil up to? *Netherworld Ways* suggests some very serious answers. It stands in the tradition of C.S. Lewis' classic *The Screwtape Letters* and Peter Kreeft's *The Snakebite Letters*. Lewis' purpose was to demonstrate how Lucifer and his minions work to subvert human souls. Kreeft's work has a somewhat different focus, one reflected in his book's subtitle, *Devilishly Devious Secrets for Subverting Society as Taught in Tempter's Training School*. His focus concerns how the Tempter works to undermine and subvert humanity on a societal and cultural scale. While both authors were dead serious in their purpose, they used the epistolary approach which allowed them to write in a comic style at once both engaging and winning. My purpose, in *Netherworld Ways,* has been to take the story a step further than either Lewis or Kreeft did, to consider the nature and condition, *the ways*, of a world in which Satan achieves pre-eminence. However, unlike those authors, I've chosen to dispense with the epistolary approach and use a straight narrative method to tell the present story, because of my distinct difference in purpose.

If one finds that Satan's netherworld and our own seem at times to almost blend into mirror images of one another, that blending is not by chance. It reflects the fact that our world has been and will continue to be one in which The Lamb and The Beast do battle for our souls and the results of those battles, the fruits of good and evil, are regularly visible around us. Netherworld is a world where there is no golden rule, no forgiveness, no help, no sensitivity, no compassion, no love – the nonsense, nothing world that men and women create when they choose to turn away and deny their God and Savior. It is the world created by those who claim to have banished or killed God, for our liberation and good. They are blind to the fallacy in their thinking, *for if they will kill God, they will feel free to destroy anything and kill anyone they wish.*

Readers will find that the narrator in *Netherworld Ways* is never named. This is intentional. As his familiar, Faust, tells him, "names have no meaning here." Individuality is extinct. From one angle, our *Netherworld* narrator might be seen as everyman, everyman because he has every man's character, which is little to no character at all. He is emblematic of today's souls who are easily seduced by their own self-deceptions and self-delusions, and who are notably unprepared to meet or fend off the Deceiver's subterfuges and subversions, let alone his direct attacks. Our narrator is a creature who has lived a chaotic existence, devoid of values beyond those of narcissistic self-service, self-pleasure, and self-aggrandizement, even though he clothes his choices in high-sounding intellectual rhetoric and wraps his purposes in the tissue paper of long overdue, modern, liberating reforms. He is one who damages, maims, even destroys others' lives. His recklessness has left him blind, deaf, and – yes – intellectually stupid. He fails to realize that his enemy is not his enemy, but his redeemer.

Though some aspects of the narrator's character seem to suggest he is everyman, other elements suggest he is closer to the educated elite that dominate today's Western thinking and societies. Captivated by radical ideas, a megalomaniacal faith that they can recreate human nature by politico-social engineering, and a host of dubious assumptions, they have striven to remake the world in their own image – without examining what image that is. (As the blind anthropologist once pontificated, "man is the measure of all things!" His waggish, but very astute, listener returned, "but which of all the men in the world do we use for that measure?")

Some few, after reviewing the narrator's life, have suggested he seems unjustly consigned to Hell, that his sins – such as they are – are personal and limited, not the sins of a serial killer or the carnage of a mass murdering political leader. That suggestion, first, misses a central fact about Hell: people are *not* consigned there by a heavenly judge. As Faust succinctly puts it, "You don't get sent here.... You come bearing the shadow of your former life over your shoulders, having discovered the way all by your perverse self." The suggestion that the narrator has been unjustly consigned is perhaps reflective of the moral decline and confusion rampant in our time, because of the refusal to believe there is any true North on our moral compass. Adultery, casual legal murder, dishonesty, betrayal, the covetousness of rampant materialism, the dishonoring of our closest human relationships, have been relegated to the status of modest character flaws, rather than deeply damaging, even at times life destroying actions.

While the narrator has made a muck of his own personal life, we should not miss the fact that he has contributed to mucking up the world in general with his dubious theories and destructive ideas. We should not miss the obvious fact that ideas have consequences, at times devastating consequences. The communism of Marx and Engels had the consequence of resulting in the destruction of over a hundred million human lives. Margaret Sanger's and Alfred Kinsey's carefully planned and executed sexual revolution has added tens of millions of completely innocent infant lives to the casualty list. Advocates of eugenic or genetic purity have contributed their victims under the justification of improving humanity, reducing poverty, and preventing stunted, suffering lives. These and a multitude more have sought to think like God and have ended in making the fatal mistake of believing they can do it better. Plunging ahead with what they think are the best of intentions they follow their self-righteous and self-serving egos, blind to the ancient adage that if humanity can get something wrong, it will!

The history of the last three centuries is emblematic of the labors of the "philosopher elite." They have declared themselves the philosopher-captains of our fate, asserted they are *now* in charge and will determine what happens. They have cast off the hawsers that moored our existence in harbor and set to sea without charts and compass, sextant or GPS – claiming instruments of their own making would produce better results. Their efforts have proven a strange and dangerous way to travel over restless waters, beset by massive storms, and alive with multitudes of monsters. The result: they have made a major muck of it and left us adrift and at the mercy of ideological madmen and their ignorant, but violent armed forces.

Today's electronic media with their chattering class - a class that can't think much beyond the present and that finds little, if any, value in the lessons of the past - dominate debate. We find ourselves standing in a sham Eden of our own creation, acting like we are gods and like we can distinguish good and evil. We listen daily to a cacophony of ridiculous hype concerning our power, intellect, unlimited potential, and coming self-realization, but when we begin to see through these frauds, we find behind them only the meaninglessness, the nothingness, the archetypal wasteland and its abyss that have always been there. And when we whisper - *is anyone in charge here?* - no one answers.

Our narrator, true only to his delusions and refusing to recognize the tenor and trend of his Netherworld experience, continues to hope that his circumstances will improve, that someone will appear to set things right, that as a bright new arrival, he will receive the recognition he rightly deserves: a commanding post in the new order. Such hope dies hard, even in hell, but when it dies, it dies a pathetic death. That spiritual death – and the story's close in which it is embodied - may disappoint some, but the characters and their actions demand it. In hell, there are no happy endings. Our anonymous narrator has ignored his chance at life, has chosen to reject his Creator, and that Creator, who loved him, has honored that choice. The day of our narrator's visitation has come and is now long past. He has failed to avail himself, even at the moment of death, of God's final offer of divine mercy. The despair that dogs the death march of the last scene and the narrator's end grow naturally from the characters and their actions. It is an ending somewhat reminiscent of Aldous Huxley's classic *Brave New World,* another story in which the "personalities," if they could be called that, are so devoid of true character that the tale ends with a whimper: the Savage's suicide, his mother's euthanasia, and Bernard Marx, the squalid victim of chemical imbalances at his birth, coming to nothing. Characters without real character come to nothing in a world without purpose, significance, or meaning.

In our age, it is easy to mock Satan, to belittle him, and to reduce him to a caricature. It is easy, but not wise, not wise because of the intense suffering and death that face us when we become the brunt of his sophisticated plots, subtle lies, and devious strategies. We have long known Satan's character, how he works on his victims, how he plays with them in his own rendition of "cat-and-mouse," and how he exploits their weaknesses to undermine and overcome all their defenses. To be caught in his nets and to suffer in his claws is no more entertaining than to be a victim in one of too many brave new worlds, a Nazi death camp, a Soviet Gulag, or a rabid jihad. Thus it is that the reader will find the tone more serious in *Netherworld Ways,* entertaining, yes, but less comic than *The Screwtape Letters.* This is no reflection on Lewis or Kreeft, for they were dealing with the present world in which hope, the possibility of redemption, exists. Netherworld is a different realm, a realm devoid of faith, hope, and love.

NETHERNOTES

[1] Genesis 19:1-11.

[2] Romans 7:21-24.

[3] Matthew 4:1-11.

[4] Genesis 3:4-5.

[5] Luke 4:1-13.

[6] The full English text of Nietzsche's parable, *The Madman*, follows: "Have you ever heard of the madman who on a bright morning lighted a lantern and ran to the market-place calling out unceasingly: "I seek God! I seek God!" As there were many people standing about who did not believe in God, he caused a great deal of amusement. Why? Is he lost? said one. Has he strayed away like a child? said another. Or does he keep himself hidden? Is he afraid of us? Has he taken a sea voyage? Has he emigrated? – the people cried out laughingly, all in a hubbub.

The insane man jumped into their midst and transfixed them with his glances. "Where is God gone?" he called out. "I mean to tell you! *We have killed him,* you and I! We are all his murderers! But how have we done it? How were we able to drink up the sea? Who gave us the sponge to wipe away the whole horizon? What did we do when we loosened this earth from its sun? Whither does it now move? Whither do we move? Away from all suns? Do we not dash on unceasingly? Backwards, sideways, forwards, in all directions? Is there still an above and below? Do we not stray, as through infinite nothingness? Does not empty space breathe upon us? Has it not become colder? Does not night come on continually, darker and darker? Shall we not have to light lanterns in the morning? Do we not hear the noise of the grave-diggers who are burying God? Do we not smell the divine putrefaction? – for even Gods putrefy! God is dead! God remains dead! And we have killed him!

How shall we console ourselves, the most murderous of all murderers? The holiest and the mightiest that the world has hitherto possessed has bled to death under our knife – who will wipe the blood from us? With what water could we cleanse ourselves? What lustrums, what sacred games shall we have to devise? Is not the magnitude of this deed too great for us? Shall we not ourselves have to become Gods, merely to seem worthy of it? There never was a greater event – and on account of it, all who are born after us belong to a higher history than any history hitherto!" Here the madman was silent and looked again at his hearers; they also were silent and looked at him in surprise.

At last he threw his lantern on the ground, so that it broke in pieces and was extinguished. "I come too early," he then said. "I am not yet at the right time. This prodigious event is still on its way, and is traveling – it has not yet reached men's ears. Lightning and thunder need time, the light of the stars needs time, deeds need time, even after they are done, to be seen and heard. This deed is as yet further from them than the furthest star – and yet they have done it themselves!" It is further stated that the madman made his way into different churches on the same day, and there intoned his *Requiem aeternam deo*. When led out and called to account, he always gave the reply: "What are these churches now, if they are not the tombs and monuments of God?"

[7]Deut.30:11-14; Isaiah 30:19-21, Romans 10:5-8.

[8]Lest readers think that the author is being a misogynist, they should recognize the text of Stopheles' "Rant in *F* Sharp" is a collage of actual pronouncements made by late 20th century radical and Marxist Feminists, such as Beauvoir, Bernard, *et al.*

www.ingramcontent.com/pod-product-compliance
Lightning Source LLC
LaVergne TN
LVHW011349080426
835511LV00005B/203